T0116839

PATRIOT SON:

MEMOIRS *of* A VETERAN

by

Gary Smith

Order this book online at www.trafford.com
or email orders@trafford.com

Most Trafford titles are also available at major online book retailers.

Printed in the United States of America.

ISBN: 978-1-4269-9335-0 (sc)
ISBN: 978-1-4269-9336-7 (e)

Trafford rev. 10/13/2011

 www.trafford.com

North America & international
toll-free: 1 888 232 4444 (USA & Canada)
phone: 250 383 6864 ♦ fax: 812 355 4082

Introduction

This account is a chronological map of my life. Beginning in a small, but vibrant central Iowa city, the story reveals the driving forces that lead me to choose the adventurous and nomadic life of a soldier and his family.

Included in the first few chapters of this memoir are life experiences from high school, college, and events leading up to my enlistment in the US Army. The story then takes my family and I through various assignments across the globe, documenting anything humorous or unusual, and describing my associations with coworkers. Letters to and from loved ones back home in 1990 and '91 during Desert Shield and Desert Storm reveal the fears that my wife and daughters faced and expressed daily that I may never come back to them; at least the way they knew me.

Additionally, I invited a close friend to travel to Washington, DC to confront the demons that have haunted him since the war in Vietnam, by standing next to the black marble wall of the Vietnam Memorial. At the last minute, Pete backed out, citing an uncontrollable fear of reopening old wounds. I did the next best thing; I interviewed him for two days about his experiences and compiled them in a passage dedicated to him and all the Vietnam vets who have never been able to return.

After retiring from the US Army in 1992, I studied to become a teacher. In 1996, I began that second life journey. Unfortunately, near the end of my fifteenth year in the classroom, my life hit a snag due to unforeseen complications from the affliction known as Gulf War Syndrome. My choice was clear: retire with dignity, or continue to explain away changes in my moods and behaviors. The latter could have had devastating consequences in working with children.

Patriot Son: Memoirs of a Veteran also represents a call to stand and serve either in the military or the classroom. To make a difference in the lives of others. However, not everyone would share these emotions. These are personal commitments.

Contents

1. The End of Another Era

The incessant buzzing of the alarm clock dragged me out of a deep sleep at 5 AM, just as it has for the better part of the past forty some years. The thought of a failed electric alarm clock drove me to use a battery powered one early in my adulthood. Fear of the electricity going out in the middle of the night lead to a domino effect of being late for work, facing supervisory chastisement, and having an overall crappy day.

My daily routine began with a trip to the bathroom, then grabbing a towel and heading out the back door to swim a few quick laps in the pool. The latter was a luxury that came with the house in Vidalia. Unfortunately, the predawn moonlight swims were not as inviting between mid October until almost the first week of April in southeast Georgia. No Polar Bear Club members in this family.

Quick check for wallet, cell phone, and oh yeah, glasses. Car keys, a go-cup of ice water and a breakfast bar in hand, I crawl behind the wheel of my Toyota Camry, back out of the garage, aim down the street east toward Tattnall County. The trip to Glennville Middle School took roughly forty seven minutes door to door depending on traffic and weather conditions. At one time, I calculated how many miles I'd driven just to and from the various schools I'd taught at in Tattnall County. It was more than seven thousand miles during a hundred and eighty day school year. Multiplied by the eleven years I've taught in Tattnall County, it came to a grand total of 73,260 miles. PTO meetings, sports events, and other school activities always added to that figure.

The morning of 8 May, 2011 held a more disturbing importance for me than did most of the daily drives to school. I had been emotionally wrestling with notion of retiring for several weeks prior. Marie retired from nursing nearly two years ago. Financially, we were still on solid ground. From time to time, I'd joke with her about my retiring from teaching.

"You've already retired once," she'd rationalize. "We just can't afford for you to retire right now. You need to stay in the classroom another five years. That way, retirement and social security will both be higher."

The mere thought of it saddened and depressed me. Look at me. I've aged. I'm not as young as I used to be. It's difficult and sometimes impossible to maintain a good attitude about teaching, a job I've loved for the past fifteen years. I've often prided myself as being well-respected by both students and staff. Back in '96, I made a promise to myself to reach at least one student per school year. If I reached that goal, I'd done my job. That goal has been reached and surpassed many times over. Lately, however, I've fought uncontrollable urges to lash out at students for minor infractions like talking in class or not paying attention. Something wasn't right.

The secrets of life are not amassed wealth or possessions, but rather happiness and contentment. Lord knows, careers in the military and in the field of education would never bring monetary wealth, but provide security and satisfaction. I was content, though. I've raised two wonderful children and had a loving and supportive wife through it all.

Whether by deliberate design or mere chance, I felt it was time to go. Teaching has been very rewarding; watching young minds grow and mature into young adulthood has more than honored my earlier goal of reaching at least one student in a school year.

Things just weren't the same, though. I grew quicker to anger. Important issues regarding classroom supervision were easily overlooked or forgotten altogether. In 1992 after I retired from the Army, I was diagnosed by the Veterans Administration with several symptoms of Gulf War Syndrome: chronic fatigue, joint pain, irritability, sleep apnea, just to name a few. For several years, I have denied the existence of these problems, dismissing them as something I could take care of by getting more sleep, exercise more often, and eating healthier.

Day after day these annoying and painful remnants of the Gulf War crept into every aspect of my physical and emotional being. It became increasingly difficult to maintain a professional balance with my peers, my superiors, and the wonderful kids I was in charge of teaching and nurturing. I was like an ogre with these kids. Impatience and intolerance of the slightest noise in a classroom full of middle school kids became a normal yet dangerous part of my daily classroom management routine.

Teacher burnout, for lack of a better label for it, is no more unusual than burnout in any other profession. It's a lot like writer's block. You know what you want to say or do, but it never quite comes out the way you intended. Hurtful sarcasm toward students and unreliability to peers and administration is not the way to perform your duties.

Yes, it was time to go. Time to just walk away. The following is a copy of the letter of intent to retire I submitted to my principal, Lisa Turner, today. Painful all by themselves, I excluded all the personal and medical reasons conflicting with my desire to continue teaching:

To: Lisa Turner, Principal
       Glennville Middle School
From: Gary Smith
       SPEd Teacher, Glennville Middle School
Date: May 8, 2011
Subject: Letter of Intent to Retire

Mrs. Turner,

I have applied for retirement through the Teacher's Retirement System of Georgia, effective May 31, 2011. I have also contacted MaryAnn Waters at the Tattnall County Board of Education office to advise me in this matter.

Sincerely,
Gary Smith

Marie already knew how I felt, how I was hurting. We'd discussed what I had planned to do that day. She left it up to me.

"We'll make it," she reassured me.

My mind was racing that night when I arrived at home. I thought about where Marie and I were going from there, and where we'd been the last forty years. What was the driving force that lead me to a career in the army, and how was it to affect my life as well as my family's?

2. The Year of the Hawk

I'd have to say that during most of my senior year at Marshalltown High, I was a dreamer. I never thought a lot about a secure future for myself, much less for a family. I also never pictured myself as a family man. Plenty of time for that. I was having too much fun growing up.

I was deeply involved in high school sports. Oh, not as a player; as a spectator. I wouldn't be caught missing a home game of any sport, and even attended some out of town games. That's where all the action was. You see, part of fitting in with peer groups meant acting like an idiot in front of the right people. Act drunk and swagger. Say witty things like, "All I did was pinch her on the butt accidentally and she begged me to go out with her." Or, you could spread the word that the biggest, meanest, and toughest guy in school was a weanie, and that you aim to hunt him down and hurt him, because he's nothing. Actions like these all seem to give you the power to win and influence new and important friends. Sort of fit in.

It always seemed, though, that after I'd leave a game to go home, the desire for recognition would diminish when I was alone. I would sink back into my own dream world and analyze what I'd said and done earlier. Yeah, I could have taken that girl out, but she would never talk to me. Yeah, I could have hunted that big guy down and beat him up, but I was too afraid. I could have done a lot of things. It was okay to fantasize about things like that, but for me, words spoke much louder than actions. Was this a gift, a curse, or something of a phase that would disappear like pimples?

The days melted into months, then at last, graduation day was near. I felt that if I remained a student there much longer, the entire faculty would chip in and buy me a one way ticket to somewhere in Montana. High school and I didn't exactly get along too well. The social benefits of being a senior interested me far more than the regimentation. My final grade point average had to have been an all time low. A one point two GPA wasn't exactly conducive to getting admitted to the college of your choice.

The big day finally arrived. Plans for travel and college for some of the graduating seniors had been made. Year books were signed with best wishes, good luck, and lines like, *to the cutest guy in biology class.*

The Marshalltown High School graduating class of '68 stood restlessly in single file in the hallway that began in the main lobby outside the principal's office, wound around by the cafeteria, and opened all the way down to the auditorium where the graduation ceremony was to be held. Looking up and down the long navy blue line of caps and gowns, I was saddened by the distinct possibility of never seeing these people again, and further saddened by the fact that I'd grown sort of close to some. On the other hand, there were some that I could certainly live just fine without. I wondered if anyone there felt the same way I did.

The minute had finally arrived. The moment of truth. Word was whispered down the long blue line to move out quietly and smartly, and for God's sake not to forget to put the navy blue and red tassel on the right side of the mortar board. It must have been a sight to behold for all those proud parents to watch their young fledglings about to take on the world, file into the auditorium to their seats.

The 365 members of the Class of '68 listening to a dozen or so boring speeches, thankful that the dome roofed gym had been transformed into an air conditioned auditorium. It had been unusually hot that June afternoon. All the speakers were professional people: doctors, lawyers, city councilmen, and educators. They all had about the same advice for us. We were congratulated on all the outstanding achievements of the past twelve years (how the hell would they know?). We had prepared ourselves well to meet the ugly world head-on. *Come on! Hurry up! Lots of parties to go to tonight!* Here we go. Okay, I'm next.

"Gary Smith," the assistant principal's unmistakable voice boomed over the public address system. I didn't like that guy since he had threatened to suspend me for fighting in the hallway between classes earlier this year. I tried to nail some jock who pushed me against my locker, and got clocked pretty good for my trouble. The assistant principal caught us as I was pushing the guy back, so I looked the guiltiest.

I marched stiffly across the stage, clicking my heels together, as I stopped directly in front of the general and saluted him smartly. My eyes stared straight ahead as he pinned the medal on my chest. The general returned my salute as I turned to march quickly off the stage and down the steps to my seat. I glanced proudly down at the medal. It was gone! What the....?

That was the weirdest feeling I'd ever experienced. It was so real. Several times as I was growing up, I would slip off into a daydream, thinking I was some sort of superhero, but it was always a momentary lapse into my dream world. Saluting the assistant principal seemed more of a reality than a delusion. Glancing down at in my right hand, I saw the rolled up diploma. It was only a delusion.

Finding my assigned chair, I sat down and cautiously peered around to determine if anyone was looking at me and wondering why the hell I saluted that guy. But, no one was looking my way. Boy, what a relief. That would've been real hard to explain.

I'd done it. I'd succeeded in the seemingly impossible task of completing high school. Somehow, finishing in the top ninety-five percent of my senior class didn't seem all that bad. My fellow classmates and I reminded each other of that fact as we milled around outside in the shade of the giant dome of the gym roof.

Tearfully proud moms hugged and kissed their young graduates as puffed-chested dads stood nearby. Teenagers reminded parents of party plans.

" Don't stay out too late," mothers would caution.

"And please be careful," fathers would offer a stern warning, like mine always did. *No liquor!* That's all my dad would ever say when I went out. I'd ask to borrow the car, and all he would say was, *No liquor!*

The summer of '68 was a maturing time for me. I took a job working for minimum wage ($1.35 an hour) at Clifton's, a major supermarket in Marshalltown. That's when I met Gilda Daniels. Gilda wasn't a dainty lady by any means. She stood a good six feet tall, skin like leather, and spoke with a cigarette voice deeper than most men's. She always came into the store with her long time friend, a tall, lanky figure of a man by the name of Pink Southard. Pink worked for a local construction company and always wore a chrome hard hat monogrammed with the initials "PS" , and dirty work clothes to the store. Pink and Gilda were and odd pair, but they'd always find time to chat with my partner in crime, Harley Phillips, and me, no matter how busy the store was. I recall one day Gilda brought in some homemade caribou sausage for Harley and me that she'd brought back from one of her sojourns to Alaska.

One mid-August night, Harley and I were 'scooping the loop,' up Main Street to Third Avenue, down Third Avenue to the A&W, and back again. We each had a cold beer on the seat between our legs, out of sight of the cops. I guzzled the remainder of mine down and tossed the empty can out the window. No sweat, I thought. Nobody'd ever see it.

The next day I was working in the store when Gilda came in. She came through the line I was bagging on, and with all the grace of a perfect hostess, she offered, "I've got some great venison steaks that will just melt in your mouth. How would you and Harley like to come over tonight and share them with Pink and me?" Not really knowing how to answer such an invitation, I accepted.

"Good, we'll expect you about six, then"

"I don't get off until six. How about six-thirty?"

"Six-thirty will be just fine," she offered. "See you then."

At six twenty-seven, Harley and I pulled up in front of Gilda's house, a small frame job at the end of a tree-lined street on the north edge of town. Gilda greeted us as we walked up the steps. The pungent aroma of steaks frying in the kitchen left us with mounting anticipation for the delicious meal that was to come.

"Come on in and set yourselves down," Gilda said. "Would you guys care for a beer?"

"Oh, no thanks," I replied. Harley's and my eyes met, both of us wondering what was going on. "We don't drink."

"Oh hogwash!" Gilda roared, handing each of us a cold beer. "Now drink 'em. That's it, drink 'em all down."

We obediently chugged the beers down, spilling some of it on our chins. As I wiped off my mouth with the palm of my hand, I noticed Pink standing in the kitchen doorway, splitting a gut trying to keep from laughing out loud. He simply couldn't contain himself any longer, and burst out laughing. With that, Gilda shooed him into the kitchen with a cold stare.

"Okay, guys," Gilda replied with diminished wrath in her voice. Which one of you threw the beer can out the window on Third Avenue last night?"

Dead silence. We were squirming now. Shit, how'd she know?

"Okay, boys," she continued calmly, "the beer can bounced off the street, hit my windshield, and put about a six-inch crack along the bottom. I wrote down your license number. Oh, I've got friends in the police department."

"Isn't that your dad's car out front, Harley?" The old girl had us cold. She was really slick. I really didn't have a clue that the beer can bounced up and hit the car behind us.

Gilda didn't make us pay for the damage to the windshield, but she sure put the fear of God in us about throwing stuff out of car windows. After Harley and I made our apologies, promising never to pull a stunt like that again, we dined sumptuously on venison steaks that night. That was Gilda Daniels, and how she helped me mature a little that summer.

The summer of '68 turned into fall. Time seemed to stand still, but so did the war in Vietnam. Every evening, I would watch intently as the six o'clock news brought yet another development in the tiresome fighting. There was a lot of commentary in the news broadcasts about something called Tet. The reporters gave it names like *Lunar New Year* and *Year of the Monkey.* Those were meaningless words to me then. They were supposed to represent some sort of religious holidays in Southeast Asia. Earlier in the year, there was a big offensive in Saigon by North Vietnamese troops and Viet Cong forces. This was labeled by the US Military as Tet Offensive, the biggest and bloodiest battle of 1968.

The news media kept calling the Viet Cong soldiers 'Charlie'. Weird name. As time went along, and the more newscasts about the war I watched on TV, the more sense they began to make. *Viet Cong…Charlie Cong. Shorten it and you have Charlie.*

I began to show a special interest in the casualty figures. When Peter Jennings or Roger Mudd would spout statistics on the North Vietnamese dead, I would think maybe the United States was going to win this war. However, when they showed bloody film clips of guys my age from time to time, I even heard them scream in agony right there on the six o'clock news. I thought, damn! There's got to be a way to end this stupid war! And for fleeting moments, I even entertained thoughts of joining the military and becoming a vital part of it all. Maybe even helping change the course of the war.

Becoming more drawn into the politics of the war, I recalled some of the speeches President Johnson had made during his earlier State of the Union addresses, such as why we were in Vietnam, and what the cost may be, both in human lives and tax dollars.

"I have ordered to Vietnam forces that will nearly double our fighting strength almost immediately. Additional forces will be needed later and will be sent as requested," I remember LBJ announcing on TV back in '65. This action almost doubled the monthly draft call, but young American men weren't exactly beating down the doors at the local draft board. Johnson also cautioned that taxes would most assuredly be raised, but the biggest tragedy of the war was the inevitable human sacrifice.

America had been involved in the war in Vietnam for years, and the reasons why still remained quite ambiguous to me. One sound rationalization would be to improve relations with the government of South Vietnam, but a good foreign policy base was a concept beyond my comprehension. Somehow, I doubted that the American public would sit still for that reasoning for very much longer. Achieving peace in Southeast Asia was another possibility. President Johnson had stated in past addresses to the nation that, during his lifetime through two world wars and the Korean Conflict--Americans had gone to far-off lands to fight for freedom, and that we had learned at a terribly brutal cost that retreat does not bring safety and weakness does not bring peace. So peace had to be the most valid reason young men were fighting and dying in that place. From my standpoint, that was acceptable. But what about the people who had lost sons, husbands , and fathers in that undeclared war? How did they feel about those reasons? Was it unobjectionable to them that their loved ones died fighting for peace on foreign soil? Those and other burning questions could only be answered by someone who has been there. For those who have fought for it, freedom has a flavor the protected will know.

Mom had gone through that anguish during World War II. Dad was a tank driver in Patton's Spearhead Division. During the Battle of the Bulge, he had suffered a great deal of emotional pain, seeing the lives of close friends snuffed out in that major battle to rid Europe of Nazi tyranny. Dad kept this torment very private for several years after the war. Mom used to tell us kids about some of the things that had happened to Dad during the war. At a very young age, I vaguely recall that he had nightmares about the war, but I never fully understood, until reaching adolescence, the impact the war had on his life--the same suffering that would linger with the survivors of the Vietnam war and their families.

The days had become shorter, and the first hues of autumn began to assert themselves in the trees. Once again, the lines of yellow school buses paraded down city streets, stopping in front of schools to disgorge streams of shouting children, eager to meet the new school year head-on. Seeing those kids so willing and excited to take on the drudgery of the next nine months (plus the pure social aspect of it all) I saw it as a fresh start, and thought about going on to college. Maybe it wouldn't be like high school.

The last few days of registration at Marshalltown Community College were coming to a close. Before making the decision to enroll, my mind focused on the war rather than college. Throughout my senior year in high school, I tried to convince myself that college was not the place I wanted to be; nor would I be ready for at least two more years of brain-fry . I had decided at the last minute to enroll for the fall semester at MCC because that's where all my friends would be. I didn't want to be left behind.

Registration was being conducted in the gym building of the old college. Ironically, I attended gym class in the very same building years earlier when it was part of the old Central Junior High. The old brick buildings had been renovated to serve as a college campus. The old gym hadn't changed much, though. The high arched ceiling with the exposed rafters and the caged lights hanging down between them to prevent a runaway basketball from shattering the bulbs, remained unchanged. Neither did the built-in bleachers overlooking the playing floor. They probably still held petrified wads of chewing gum underneath the edges of the seats. You could almost hear the *thud-twang* of basketballs being dribbled, and the screech of tennis shoes on the wooden floor. And that unmistakable odor that never seemed to vanish emitting from the nearby locker room.

The old gym had been converted into a registration center for new and returning MCC students. Lines of tables had been set up to allow students to register for classes and purchase textbooks. Buy books? In high school, they gave them to us. Above each table hung a sign bearing 'A-D', 'E-H' and so on. I stood there looking around like a dumb freshman trying to decipher the system when a distinguished older gentleman approached me, slightly amused by the puzzled look on my face.

"Son," he said, "if your last name begins with one of the letters you see above these tables, that is where you'll start."

"Oh yeah, thanks," I responded feeling a little embarrassed.

"You're quite welcome."

Glancing down the line to my right, I spotted the table with the 'R-U' sign above, and walked slowly towards it wondering if I really wanted to do this. I presented all the required documents for enrollment to a prim-looking lady in her mid thirties, dressed fashionably in a low cut, tight-fitting sweater and short skirt, sitting behind the table.

She glanced at me sort of sideways from behind her coke-bottle half reading glasses. Her strawberry blond hair was pulled tightly into a bun. A pencil was sticking out of it ready to be drawn like a knife. Her tongue slowing and teasingly traced the outline of her pouting lips as she turned her gaze to stare at me.

"May I help you?" she inquired in a businesslike tone. I just stood there, mouth agape, staring back at her.

"Can I help you with something?' This time she snapped rather impatiently.

"Oh, oh yeah," I stammered, somewhat ashamed that she'd probably caught me looking at her cleavage. I sure hoped she didn't think I was mentally undressing her.

"I would like to enlist…uh, I mean enroll in some classes that would help toward a degree."

"And what degree is that?" she asked, sounding a little frustrated with me.

"Business," I replied quickly. A business degree was the first thing that popped into my head. Sounded pretty good, anyway.

"A degree in business requires a solid background in mathematics. I see from your high school transcript that you had some difficulty in that area. An 'F' in freshman geometry and a 'D' in sophomore algebra. I don't see any more math courses. That's not exactly meeting the prerequisites for a business degree."

"But I can explain those grades."

"Please, don't try to explain," she reasoned. "That's what everyone says. It's all right here in your transcript. What I suggest is that you enroll in some basic core subjects and include a remedial math course to improve your grades; then , later, take some economics and business courses. You will be placed on academic probation for the first semester because of your high school grades."

"Okay, thanks for your help," I replied with a mixture of sarcasm and resignation in my voice. Academic probation? What a put-down!

"Now then, please sign here, here, and initial here," she said pointing to the appropriate places on the forms she had thrust in front of me. "You'll find the cashier's table over on the far side. You can buy the books you need at the table right next to it," she added, nodding in the direction of the bleachers.

"Thank you very much," I returned, with all the respect and sincerity taught by my upbringing. I then wove my way over to the bleachers with tuition forms, class schedules, and checkbook in hand. I wrote out the check for the first semester's tuition and fees, handing it to the cashier. I hated spending all that money. Two hundred and forty-five dollars was pretty much my life savings. Stepping off to the corner, I balanced my checkbook, discovering I had barely enough gas money for the rest of the week. That is, if I hadn't made any serious errors in figuring. It was a damn good thing that I still lived with my parents.

Looking over my class schedule, I noticed she had me down for Bernie Manchester's English Literature course at seven-thirty on Monday, Wednesday, and Friday mornings. I'd heard about him. This didn't look too good. Professor Manchester was a huge and imposing bald-headed man with the demeanor of a grizzly bear. Being of Scottish ancestry, he loved to recite old Scottish poems, complete with a thick brogue. Later, I would learn that if old Bernie gave a writing assignment of a short story depicting a real-life experience, it better be believable. I chose to write about a little guy by the name of Elmo, from Sheboygan, Wisconsin. Well, when I got the paper back from him a few days later, there were several comments below the big red 'F' he gave me, pointing out all the grammatical errors and asking questions such as, "Have you ever been to Sheboygan, Wisconsin?" and , "Did you really know a little man named Elmo from there?" "Try harder next time," he added venomously.

The rest of my classes sounded relatively easy. Sociology would be a cinch if it was anything like the class I took in high school. Spanish 101 was also on the list. *Por favor, gracious, no comprende,* I figured I could learn to say those things.

I began the fall semester at MCC with all the enthusiasm of a new freshman. I soon found myself, however, spending more and more time in the student union. That was where all the action was. I started out just going there to take a break between classes, but that soon turned into a break during classes. One afternoon, while on one of my breaks, I ran into Dave Hansen, an old friend from high school.

"Hey man, how's it going?" he yelled across the crowded union. "I thought you had soc this morning."

"I did, but I got bored, so here I am," I hollered back, making my way across the crowded room to where Dave was standing.

He had to raise his voice to be heard over the din in the union lounge, as he started the same lecture I'd heard so many times from him.

"You know," he began," if you don't get your mind where it belongs, you're gonna blow it."

"Can't help it," I confessed. "I just decided at the last minute to register. I didn't do so good in high school, and this place is really getting to be a pain in the butt. I've been thinking a lot about Vietnam, and I need some answers, but not the answers some know-it-all recruiter wants to give me. I just wasn't ready for college, but I don't know if I'm ready to enlist."

"Tell you what," Dave suggested, "let's go to the coffee house in the basement of the library uptown tonight. There's usually something happening every night there. Some MCC teachers put this thing together last fall to give students a place to talk about politics, the war, sex, drugs, or anything else you can't talk to your folks about. What do you say?"

"Oh, I don't know...sitting around talking to a bunch of hippies?"

"It's not all that bad," he replied. "There are some, but they sort of add to the atmosphere. Really some pretty good discussions. Think you'll like it. How's eight o'clock sound?"

"I'll just meet you there at eight."

"Right, Bud, see you tonight." Dave was okay, but he was the only person that ever called me 'Bud.'

The city library was a beautiful old stone building built sometime back in the 20's. Its three floors held an unimaginable amount of literary works. I remember when I was a kid living on a farm outside of Gilman about fifteen miles east of Marshalltown, my brother and two older sisters would go up to the third floor for story hour whenever my family would come to town on a Saturday. Even back in junior high, which is now the MCC main campus, it was one of my favorite places to go and hang out, escaping into a fantasy world created by simply reading a book. I found a place to park behind the old building and entered through the basement door.

The coffee house was a large room donated by the library for college students to hang out at night. One stipulation the library staff made was that the place had to be kept clean. Also, if there were any problems whatsoever, that would be the end of the coffee house. The soft glow of candlelight lit up each corner of the room. Over-stuffed pillows and beanbag chairs were scattered randomly around the room, lending to a relaxed atmosphere of free discussion. There were only about half a dozen young people there, all listening intently to a man in his early thirties talking about a book I'd never read. He was wearing a tweed sport coat over a white T-shirt, and faded blue jeans.

I walked in quietly and sat down on a pillow near the door. Scanning the room for Dave, I found him sitting on the far side of the room next to a girl with short brown hair, dressed in a white turtleneck sweater and tight blue jeans. Dave waved discreetly and smiled when he spotted me. I returned the smile, glancing at the girl sitting next to Dave. She was smiling at me. She sure did look familiar. Where have I seen her before, I wondered?

Later, the small crowd broke into discussion groups to talk about the social ills of the world. Dave and I got into the same group, along with the girl with the sweet smile, whom he introduced to me. I've always been terrible with names the first time I meet someone, but I remembered right away that her name Marie. Nice name. Nice face. Cute smile. She filled out the jeans and sweater she was wearing quite nicely. I felt myself being attracted to her in a way that could only be described as my needing some type of fulfillment. Not necessarily a lustful fulfillment, but for a companionship that was lacking in my life.

We all three left the coffee house around nine-thirty that evening. Marie, Dave , and I were standing in the parking lot in the chill October night air saying our good-nights. He leaned over and kissed Marie affectionately on the lips.

"Hey, would you mind if I kissed her, too?" I called after Dave walking toward his car with Marie. I didn't even think about what I was saying; I just blurted it out.

"Fine with me," Dave replied unexpectedly. "Why don't you ask her?"

As I approached Marie, I was wondering what the hell made me say something so stupid. She was smiling the same way she had in the coffee house. As if in slow motion, we kissed. I had never been kissed like that before.

"Hope to see you again sometime, okay?" I managed to say.

"Maybe," she replied, still smiling.

I didn't see Marie very often after that night. I tried to stay clear, because I sort of thought she was Dave's girlfriend. We did run into each other from time to time, whenever she was in town. She was attending Area Six Community College in Fort Dodge, about ninety miles away. She drove a white '66 Mustang convertible that was very easy to spot in the nightly loop traffic. It had a red leather interior with a pair of homemade rose-tinted wire rimmed sunglasses hanging from the rear-view mirror. One night, I spotted Marie as I was driving the loop. That white Mustang really stood out. We both pulled over, and I got into her car on the passenger side.

"Wanna ride around for a while? I asked, still believing she was Dave's girl.

"Sure, let's go," she said. "Let's put the top down." She had that same smile on her face; the one that intrigued me since we met. Not a suggestive smile, just a happy smile, a 'glad to see you' smile.

Down came the top, and off we drove, down towards Third Avenue and the A&W. Tired of driving the loop, we headed north out of town to Union Grove Lake, about fifteen miles away. It was a clear moonlit night. A bit on the chilly side, but perfect for a romantic drive in the country.

We drove slowly down the steep gravel road and parked at the edge of the lake. With a full October moon in our faces, we sat watching moon beams dance across the rippling waters. Night insects chirped in the grass and the trees around the car. It was a beautiful night. I looked at Marie sitting beside me. She had that familiar smile on her face, a sort of beaming -all-over smile. Leaning toward each other in the bucket seats, our lips met in passionate longing. Not a brief kiss as before, but with deep, lasting feeling.

"It's getting late," I cautioned feeling a bit guilty. "We'd better get back to town."

"I guess you're right," Marie agreed hesitantly. "I have some work I have to get done for tomorrow."

We didn't talk much all the way back to Marshalltown. The question kept coming up in my mind--was she Dave's girlfriend? I felt that Marie and I had so much to give each other. She dropped me off at my car, and we said good night.

"Please write me?" she said, writing her address on a scrap of paper and handing it to me.

"Write me too?" I returned, scribbling my address down and slipping it into her hand, We wouldn't see each other for several months after that night.

Several students at MCC that fall semester were trying to earn extra cash by typing term papers for classmates. Sounded like a pretty sure way of making things last until payday, so I thought I'd give it a shot. My sister Bette had left behind and old Smith-Corona college model typewriter when she got married, so I made up a few signs to hang up around campus, advertising my new enterprise. Only two bucks a page, the signs said. Not being an expert typist, I only promised a forty-eight hour turnaround. Business was slow at first, but toward the end of the semester I was typing one, maybe two papers every night.

Things were really getting out of hand, though. I would work from five to nine every night at the store, then go home and type papers. Screw studying, I was making quite a little cash in the term paper business. My grades were in the toilet, and I would fall asleep at the damnedest times in the damnedest places. One day, I went over to Harley's apartment to study. This was ten in the morning, and figured I'd have plenty of time to get to work by five o'clock, so I closed my eyes to grab quick nap. At six-thirty, Harley came in to find me sleeping, and threw a glass of ice water in my face. When a sleeping dog is kicked, chances are he's going to come up snarling. I came up swinging. Harley stood only about five four and weighed all of a hundred and fifteen pounds, and consequently I must have scared the shit out of the poor guy.

"Hey, man, I've been trying to wake you up for over an hour!" he protested, jumping back like he'd been shot at. "The boss is real pissed at you, and your dad's even called the cops. Everybody's out looking for you!" Then is when I decided just to forego the term paper business.

More and more each day, I realized my mind was not on college, but still on the war in Vietnam. Christmas break was coming up soon, and I conceded that as long as my grades were where they were, that was it. I was not coming back. After the holidays, there were only two weeks until the end of the first semester. College would be over for me for a while. Christmas came and went, and I didn't return to MCC. My parents were furious, but in time they accepted the fact that I didn't really want to be there.

The *living room war,* or *Johnson's war* as political critiques called it, plodded on into 1969 at a snail's pace. Each time I watched a TV newscast, read a magazine article, or saw a soldier in uniform, the feelings I had about joining the military service became stronger--a powerful nagging force that shouted of patriotism. Duty, honor, country. The words of General Douglas MacArthur began to sound a lot less corny, only strengthened my desire to throw caution to the wind and enlist. But I was only eighteen years old. I wasn't supposed to make such a rash decision affecting me possibly the rest of my life. I needed more time. Time to think. Time to grow. There were mountains to climb and more wild oats to sow.

That must have been what that guy meant when he said in one of my graduation speeches, "You must be able to make life decisions on your own." I thought then that was only so much bullshit.

The thought of joining the army was a little scary to say the least. A lot of what I'd seen on the TV news and read about in newspapers and magazines was focused on the war in Vietnam. I often wondered if I enlisted , would I be sent to Vietnam never to return, or would I become a war hero. I began to be increasingly fascinated by the latter more and more. Maybe someday, but not now, not yet.

With a great sense of pride, I had registered with the local draft board in the spring of '69. Conveniently, the Selective Service Office was located right next to the recruiter's office on Linn Street across from the court house. I almost went in and enlisted one day, but reality had a weak, albeit present, practical grip on me. My folks would have coronaries if I'd gone home and told them I'd enlisted. Iowa used a lottery system for the draft. The highest average number drawn was 95, and my assigned number was 285. So, chances of my being drafted in the next year were almost nil.

3. Crossroads

Early in the spring of '69, Dave Hansen and I became actively involved in working with the youth group of a large Baptist church in town. Most members of the group were high school students, some were in college. The college kids volunteered as youth leaders. Dave had asked me to be a part of the leadership group, so there I was.

An opportunity was presented by the church council for two members of the group to travel to Mexico that summer, for the purpose of working with a missionary group from California that the church helped support. Two specific conditions had to be met, however, for those who volunteered to go. You must be a member of the church, and a recommendation by a member of the church had to be made. Having an adequate amount of influence with the church missions council, Dave had decided not to go, but put in a good word for me. Accordingly, I was selected to go on the trip.

Dave had lined up a summer job on the photography staff at the local newspaper. He showed no remorse about his decision to stay behind, although he admitted that going to Mexico would have been nice. But Dave realized that working for a newspaper would eventually give him the break he'd always dreamed of--a chance to leave his mark on the fickle world of photojournalism.

Excited about the prospects of traveling to Mexico, for whatever reasons, I willingly participated in the confirmation classes to gain membership in the church. This struck a very ironic note for me, because when I was eleven years old, my parents practically had to hog-tie and drag me in to take the same classes to join the church I grew up with in Albion. It was an ugly battle, but my folks persevered. I guess I was a little embarrassed about what my friends would think if they knew I was going to Sunday School three days a week.

The course lasted only three weeks--that is three nights a week in the pastor's study. My confirmation training culminated with baptism by immersion, a totally new experience for me. It was sort of like wetting yourself in public and feeling very proud about it.

That next Sunday, the pastor announced to the congregation the names of the would-be evangelists chosen to do the Lord's work in Mexico that summer.

"I'm very pleased to announce that the missions council has reached their decision on the Summer Evangelist selectees for the Mexico trip, " the pastor beamed from the pulpit.

"Working with the Friends of Mexico this summer will be Harold Pfieffer, Jr., son of Brother Harold Sr. and Sister Beulah Pfieffer, and one of the newest members of our flock, Gary Smith, son of Chalmer and Voda Smith of Albion. Boys, please stand and be recognized." Harold preferred to be called 'Junior', so that's what everyone called him.

Junior and I stood up and looked around at the sea of approving faces. A scattering of *amens* rose up across the crowded sanctuary. Junior's parents sat brimming with pride. Beulah gave us both a discreet fingertip wave. A couple rows behind us, I spotted Marie sitting next to Dave. I smiled at her, and she winked back, again treating me to that unforgettable smile of hers.

As we sat back down on the pew, with the limelight on us dimming, the attention of the church-goers focused once again on the pastor, who by then was gathering steam to deliver another sermon on the sins of man. This guy always had everyone's undivided attention.

Normally, I would concentrate on trying to maintain some level of alertness during a sermon. That Sunday morning, however, my mind was racing with plans for the trip to Mexico. Solutions for logistical problems such as transportation, food, lodging, and of course, money would all have to be ironed out. These problems needed attention because our departure date was only two months away. Interstate travel. International travel. Up to that point, I'd never been out of Iowa, much less out of the country. I would try and make the best of these new experiences, and maybe even reach the crossroads I'd been looking for in my life.

The pastor had wound down from the pointed sermon and announced the closing hymn. The benediction was offered with a stern warning to go forth and sin no more. The congregation filed slowly up the aisle toward the great oak doors to greet the pastor and his wife. Along the way, folks stopped to chat with friends and neighbors, wishing each other well and making plans for the traditional Sunday feast.

Junior's folks motioned him toward them, and he turned to me half-heartedly, saying, "I'll see what they want and meet you outside in a few minutes."

Shaking the pastor's hand and thanking him for another great sermon, I passed through the high oak doorway down the steps into the warm April sun. Marie and Dave were standing in the shade of the old elm tree in front of the church. I approached them, hoping she wouldn't be too upset with me for not writing her. I was never very good at writing letters.

"Hi, how've you been, Marie?" I said, shaking Dave's hand briefly, trying hard to disguise the guilt I still felt about the moonlit trip to the lake. "Good to see you again."

"Where've you been hiding lately?" she asked with a sideways glance.

"I haven't been hiding, just trying to stay ahead of the rats," I said, trying to be witty.

"Well, are they going to win?" Marie quipped.

"I'm trying to hold them off for the summer."

"So I heard." There was a hint of disappointment in her tone and expression. "Say, do you think I could go along with you guys?" she asked jokingly. Somehow, I thought she was serious. Why else would she ask a question like that?

" I don't know if that would be such a hot idea," I said looking around to see if any of the old folks heard Marie's thought-provoking request. Yeah, why not, I thought. If I had to choose between Marie Davis and Junior Pfieffer, who do you think I'd pick? Come on, let's be serious!

"I was only teasing," she admitted. Somehow, I still thought she was serious about going.

Junior descended the front steps of the church after talking to his folks and came over to where we were standing. As I watched him approach, I tried to convince myself I was not choosing between Marie and him, but rather making a decision to do great works in the mission field. If the choice had been between the two of them, it certainly would have been an easy one. Marie was far more attractive to me than he was, and old Junior had his share of problems. God sure had a sense of humor when He created him. Junior walked with a sort of slumped over, arm-swinging gait , which made him look a lot like Walter Matthau. He was short and stocky, with an over-sized nose. Also, Junior had been fighting a losing battle with acne throughout most of his adolescence, which made him terribly self-conscious. He compensated for that problem in other areas, however. He constantly demanded perfection from everyone around him, and when he didn't get his own way, he went into a real snit.

"My folks wanted to invite you to dinner today," he stated, matter-of-factly. Sometimes Junior had the tact of an armadillo. Asking me to dinner at his house in front of Marie and Dave didn't set too well with me.

"But I gotta warn you," he continued, "Witch Hazel will be there."

"Thanks anyway, maybe some other time. My folks were going to meet me at Apgar's studio to have a family picture taken." Witch Hazel? Ugh! If she would be there, I'd just as soon not. She was Junior's Aunt Hazel who looked strangely like him. Same build, same nose, and same walk. She always seemed to be at his house, especially for Sunday dinner. In her mid-fifties, she was as bossy as they come.

"Tell your folks thanks anyway," I said politely. "Junior, this is Marie Davis, a friend of mine from Melbourne, and you remember Dave Hansen."

"Yeah, Dave, good seeing you again. Nice meeting you, Marie." Junior lacked a good deal of sincerity in his tone. "Okay, Gary, your loss. See you later, then. Give me a call. I may have a line on an old bread truck we can drive to Mexico. Needs a lot of work, but my old man can do a lot of it for us."

"Tell you what, I'll give you a call Tuesday night and we'll talk about it." Watching Junior walk away, I thought to myself what a jerk he could be sometimes. He had all the politeness of a badger sometimes. Plus, I never referred to my dad as 'my old man.' It just was plain disrespectful.

The bread truck may have just solved our transportation problem. I'd have to take a closer look at it, not that I didn't trust Junior's judgement on such things. Mechanical aptitude was not one of his attributes.

I almost felt sorry for Junior, leaving him alone with Witch Hazel. What I really hated, though , was lying about my reasons for turning down one of Beulah's world-class Sunday dinners. Besides, I suspected there may be a remote chance that Marie and I could get together that afternoon. Unfortunately, that was about to change. Marie turned and walked slowly toward her Mustang, with those rose-colored glass hanging from the rear-view mirror. I walked with her, looking for a way to ask her what she was doing that later, and not upset Dave. But, before I could ask her, she sat my idea at rest.

"It was good to see you again, but I have to get back to Fort Dodge and get some studying done before tomorrow," she said. "I'll probably see you next weekend, okay?"

"Sorry you have to rush off. Maybe the three of us can get together sometime."

"Maybe…" She let her voice trail off, giving me a knowing smile.

I was relieved and disappointed at the same time, knowing that Marie and I would eventually get together without Dave around. Though a little slow on the uptake at times, I was beginning to get the picture of these two. I waved goodbye to Dave as we walked to our own cars. Someday, I thought to myself as I watched Marie drive off. Someday.

Tuesday night, I called Junior as we'd planned. He laid out the particulars of the old bread truck he'd located, but left the decision of buying it up to me, since I was more mechanically inclined. We would split the cost fifty-fifty.

Junior's discovery was located in the back lot of the Buick dealership on Third Avenue. Car dealers always keep their 'white elephants' away from public view for some reason. I guess they think if the old wrecks have anything contagious, it wouldn't spread to the newer cars. I'd take a look at its potential the next morning.

The ancient Ford step-van was an imposing symbol of a bygone era of store-to-store bread deliveries, the painted-over logo of the bakery it served so well still visible. Not quite ready to be turned into scrap metal, its previous owners graciously traded it in for a newer, more reliable model. The sagging white hulk had been moved to the graveled back lot to make room for cars and trucks that would sell faster. The right front tire had been flat for some time, evidence that a non-seller gets indefinitely ignored.

A stereotypical plaid -jacketed salesman approached as I crawled out from underneath the old truck, brushing the dust off my pant-legs and shirt sleeves. I almost laughed out loud when I saw this guy. He looked like a walking commercial for used cars.

"Beauty, isn't she ?" he offered with expectant fervor.

"Yeah, I guess so. How much are you asking?" I was probing to see how deep his nonsense would run.

"Six hundred, and I'd be giving it away at that price."

"I'll give you three-fifty for it right now if it runs." A while back, Dad taught me how to barter and never back off.

"Oh, she'll run all right," he said hopefully. He probably had his fingers crossed behind his back. "Go ahead and crank her up."

He tossed me the keys as I walked around to the driver's side, slid the door back and climbed up into the driver's seat. The interior of the old truck had a musty odor to it from sitting closed up in the sun for a while. Looking through the huge steering wheel, I noticed that all the gauges seemed to be present. I inserted the key in the ignition and switched it on. Nothing. Oh yeah, these old heaps usually had a foot-switch starter. I located the switch and stepped hard on it. The tired engine growled slowly, caught, and then died. Being nursed by the manual choke, after several attempts, the engine coughed and sputtered to life. I let it warm up slowly, not knowing what surprises the fluid levels held.

"See, what'd I tell ya?" he jubilantly yelled over the engine noise reverberating inside the empty van.

"Three-fifty," I reaffirmed as I turned the ignition off and climbed down out of the driver's seat.

"Okay, but I'm takin' quite a loss here," the salesman hesitated. "Tell you what, you look like an honest young fella, and the old girl has sat here for a while. Three-fifty it is. Lets go inside and sign the papers. I'll even have a mechanic put the spare on for you, how's that?

The transaction complete, I returned to the back lot to oversee the mechanic tightening down the last lug nut on the wheel the salesman had promised. Thanking him, I climbed back up behind the over-sized steering wheel and went through the engine starting procedures. This time, the old engine roared into life on the first try.

It was too easy. I wondered what was wrong with the old truck as I drove it off the lot and down State Street toward Junior's place. Actually, it didn't run all that bad. I was sort of proud of that old piece of rescued scrap metal. The engine purred with renewed energy, as if thankful for being liberated from the junk pile.

Junior came bounding out the back door and stopped in his tracks as I wheeled the behemoth into the Pfeiffer's driveway. He just stood there, not saying a word, scrutinizing the old truck.

"Let's get to work on it," he proclaimed as a smile of approval spread across his face.

In a few weeks, with the expert help of Junior's dad, the rusted hulk had been lovingly transformed into a road-worthy, finely tuned, personalized work of art. Sheet metal had replaced the rusted-out side panels. New tires replaced the old weather-checked tread-bare ones. The electrical system had been rewired, including a new ignition, spark plug wires, and bulbs. The list was endless.

I was amazed at how the job of getting the old truck ready for the road had snow-balled into a major operation. Junior and I painted the entire body of the truck a gleaming white. With a roller. We couldn't afford to spray it. New carpet, dark walnut paneling , an easy chair and chest of drawers were all benevolently donated by Witch Hazel. Long hours, sometimes into the night, had finally paid off. Our 'mobile home' was complete.

It was the first week of June, and our departure date was only days away. The truck had been ready for almost two weeks. During the last few weeks, I had spent countless hours working on the old truck in Junior's driveway with him and his dad. Almost every meal had been eaten at their table, and I had been treated as one of the family. I failed to realize, however, the hurt I was causing my parents. Between my job at the store, which I had quit the week before, church, and working on the truck, I rarely saw my folks. When I did, it was only long enough to change my clothes and say goodbye, heading off to Junior's house.

Outwardly, my parents understood why I was spending so much time away from home. I sensed a feeling of abandonment they had, however, about the time I was spending at the Pfeiffer's, particularly on Sunday afternoons. A son or daughter cannot possibly experience the hurt that a parent feels when made to sit out part of their child's development. All the same, Mom had trusted me to be doing what was so important to me. At one point, she and I talked at length about the trip to Mexico, and reasons why I joined the church and go into the mission field. Actually, it was quite simple. I was no different from any other teenager right out of high school. Some go on to college; some try, and some fail. It's not that they're stupid or anything, but kids have more trouble that others making life decisions.

My life had not been mapped out for me like the lives of a lot of other kids I knew. Mom and Dad went through some pretty tough times raising six kids, and extra money for frivolities such as college funds and that first car was just not in the picture. If my brother or one of my sisters wanted something bad enough, we had been taught patience, and sooner or later it would come, but only if we earned it. College was a decision Mom and Dad left to us, and if it was remotely possible, they would help with financing. Literally translated, Dad would co-sign a student loan for me, but it would be my responsibility to pay off the loan.

Mom and Dad understood for a long time my reasoning for quitting MCC-- working and saving for the trip to Mexico. They never talked about it, though. They were simply waiting for me to communicate my feelings to them. I was relieved to know they understood, but I couldn't help feeling I'd forsaken them. Until I was grown and had kids of my own, I would never fully understand how they felt.

4. The Trip

Six a.m., June 7th, came with blinding flashes of lightning and rolling thunder that seemed to have no end. When I was a kid, I always thought that thunder meant that the angels in Heaven were having a bowling tournament, and every time they bowled a strike, the lightning would crash. Brothers, sisters, aunts, uncles, and cousins usually told little kids that kind of crap to ease the fear of a thunderstorm. They would add stuff like the angels were wrestling, or God was dropping potatoes down the cellar steps.

Mom and Dad drove me to Junior's house from our home in Albion that dark and windy morning. Along the way, there were several tree limbs down in the streets, some even blocking the paths of cars. Street department and power company crews were already hard at work with chain saws, clearing up the mess the storm had left behind.

The wind had died down considerably by the time we arrived at Junior's place. Climbing out of the back seat of Dad's old Ford Galaxy, I glanced up at the sky. Heavy slate-colored overcast was slowly giving way to a line of blue sky on the western horizon. Bad weather clearing up at the last minute was always a good sign. The early morning air smelled fresh and clear, as it always does after a good rain.

I walked over to the gleaming white converted bread truck with a sense of pride and accomplishment. Droplets of water left by the storm formed strings of tiny pearls running down the sides of the freshly painted step van. The rain drops on the paint gave an aura of rebirth to the once abandoned truck. I stood back and admired the inscription I'd painted in red and blue psychedelic balloon-like letters on the side panels. It simply read, 'Friends', drawn from the purpose of the trip, to work with Friends of Mexico, a mission group out of Downey, California.

Mom walked up beside me, gently placed her hand on my arm and commented, "So this is what you've been spending so much time on." I hadn't stopped to think that this was the first time either Mom or Dad had ever seen the truck.

"Yeah, this is it. What do you think?"

"It's so…white. And big, too." I knew Mom was trying to share my sense of accomplishment, but sometimes she had a funny way of showing it. It wasn't the vehicle itself; Mom didn't know a truck from a car. That sort of thing just wasn't important in her life. She was simply sharing the pride I showed in attaining such a goal.

"Looks like you boys did a real fine job on this old," Dad commented as he came over to join us. "Yessir, a real fine job."

"Thanks, Dad," I said, actually expecting a lesser response. He'd always possessed

My parents and I stood there in the driveway looking at the truck for what seemed like an eternity, then our gazes turned to each other. Not a word was spoken, but I could tell by the looks on their faces that this day was not going to be like the first time I took off down the gravel road by our farm outside of Gilman on my bike, stayed overnight the first time with a friend, or stayed out all night without calling home. Mom's chin began to quiver, and her eyes glistened with that first revealing tear. She had every right to react that way. It must have been pretty scary for her, knowing anything could happen on the trip, together with the knowledge that I would return from Mexico a changed person. Dad simply looked at the ground, then at the street, not saying a word.

The somber mood was suddenly broken by a window being opened. Timely as always, Junior stuck his head out of his bedroom window proclaiming, "It's time! Help me load this stuff!"

Boxes of food, clothes, and other necessities were passed through the open window and loaded aboard the old truck. Amazingly, everything found an obscure hiding place. The chest of drawers was neatly packed with clothes. Cans of food and munchies for the trip were stashed in all available cubby holes. All was complete and ready to go, except for the goodbyes.

Everyone was treated to one of Beulah's country breakfasts before junior and I hit the road. I would certainly miss her cooking. As we ate, the conversation wandered back and forth from graduation, the trip to Mexico, and then on to college. The table talk, however diminished nearly as fast as the food did. Mom, bless her heart, broke the deafening silence by offering to help with the breakfast dishes. Off they went to the kitchen to share the housekeeping, and perhaps to console each other about their young men about to strike out on their own. Junior and I and our two fathers stepped out into the bright morning sunlight to make a final check of the truck.

A few minutes later, Mom and Beulah came out the back door, each carrying a small bag of sandwiches. They were both smiling broadly, so evidently whatever they talked about in the kitchen had had a soothing effect on the depression they'd both been in. That sort of made leaving a lot easier.

Mom and Dad took snapshots of Junior and me as we climbed into the truck. I took the first shift, so I cranked up the truck to let it warm up. After a few canned 'touristy' shots, we waved goodbye, and I eased the van out of the driveway and up the street. I couldn't believe it; we were actually on our way! All the months of preparation had finally come to fruition. It almost seemed like a dream, but dreams sometimes have strange endings.

The old truck had been humming right along for about an hour and a half. Everything was perfect. The weather was beautiful, and the traffic on I-35 south of Des Moines relatively light for nine o'clock on a weekday morning. Seeing a sign for a weigh station, I thought I'd better pull in, just in case. Things were running too smoothly, and as luck would have it, the weigh master instructed me over the loudspeaker to pull off the scales, park the truck, and have my papers ready. Junior and I looked at each other wide-eyed. Papers? Was he kidding?

Probably the worst thing that could've happened on the whole trip was about to materialize. Junior and I, to save a few bucks, had registered the old truck as a one-ton, instead of the required two-ton. By law, we were a ton overweight. We were charged with that plus holding a false registration. Things started to look pretty dismal. A state police car escorted us to a small town justice of the peace office just off the interstate. We paid the fine, plus court costs, then Junior called his dad, begging him to call a friend of his who worked in the county clerk's office in Marshalltown to get the proper registration and the right sticker for the license plates.

With the fine reluctantly paid, and all the necessary calls made, all we could do was wait for Junior's dad to show up with the right papers. I had settled into that thought and was trying to make the best of a screwy situation. Junior's reaction, however, was the exact opposite. Whenever something interfered with the well-oiled machinery of his life, he sometimes went off the deep end.

"I sure hope this makes you happy!" Junior blurted out as he kicked up a spray of crushed rock in the JP's driveway. "This little decision of yours just cost us a total of forty-nine dollars, plus seventeen in court costs! To top that off, we've got to wait for three hours for my old man to show up!" Junior was really working himself up into a lather. His face was red and the veins in his neck were sticking out.

"My little decision?" This time, I didn't hold back. "Listen, Bub, you and I went to the courthouse and bought the registration together, remember? Besides, your father even thought it would be okay to register the truck as a one ton, so don't give me any more of your crap! Just cool it and wait. The money's been paid, so don't sweat it."

"Well, when we run out of money, then don't you sweat it."

"What's your problem?" I could sense that his little scene was disturbing the peace and tranquility of the JP's front yard.

"I don't have a problem," Junior retorted. "I just can't stand disorder. These Iowa motor vehicle laws are ridiculous. Shit, we'll probably get stranded somewhere in Texas because of all this!"

"Junior."

"What?"

"Shut up."

"Oh, you really piss me off sometimes!"

Away he stomped, to find a nice quiet place to sit down and cool off. Good old roll-the-toothpaste-up-from-the-bottom-of-the-tube Junior. He finally showed his true colors. I often wondered what I saw in this guy; why I chose to make this trip with him. I just closed my eyes and recalled Marie's suggestion about going with us. Some day, I thought. Yes, some day we can be together.

I had just dozed off, leaning against the trunk of a big maple tree in the JP's front yard when I was startled by a horn honking. I opened my eyes to see Junior's dad pulling into the drive.

"How'd everything go, Mr. Pfeiffer? I called out to him as he emerged from his car.

"Pretty good, pretty good." Junior's dad always repeated himself like that. "I'm just thankful all this happened before you boys left Iowa, instead of at the Mexican border."

"Yes sir, me too," I agreed. That, I believe, Mr. Pfeiffer, I thought to myself, would be the end of your son as a civilized human being.

Mr. Pfeiffer had to sign some sort of power of attorney release to get the right documents for us, because we were underage. The three of us went into the JP's office to present all the new paperwork, Junior not saying a word.

With that little fiasco behind us, and no real harm done except for Junior's spirited meltdown, the three of us walked over to the truck, once more saying our farewells.

"Now, you boys write if you need anything, and don't forget to call when you get to Mexico," Junior's dad prodded.

"We will, Mr. Pfeiffer."

"Okay, Dad."

"If anything comes up along the way, don't hesitate to call."

We waved goodbye as I backed slowly out of the driveway and headed south toward the interstate. The morning, what was left of it, was clear and bright. The old truck was running well, and I was regaining the positive feelings I had had earlier about the trip.

The rest of the journey to the Mexican border was, for the most part, uneventful. An ignition wire came loose in Oklahoma, but that only delayed us for a few minutes. The hardest part about fixing it was trying to explain to Junior what the problem was. Thankful that one of us was rational, I made the repair, and we were once again on our way.

Crossing the vast plains of Texas seemed to take forever. The best speed I could coax out of the old girl was just over fifty. Listening for any rogue engine noises and unusual whining of differential gears kept me completely focused, reminding me that abusing the old truck would have a terminating effect on its operation. Whoever was in the driver's seat, it was agreed that gauges had to be constantly monitored to make sure we had a safe oil pressure, and the old girl wasn't trying to overheat.

The steady drone of the old six cylinder engine drowned out any chance for an intelligible conversation, which was fine with me. Talking to Junior about anything of importance was like arguing with yourself in the mirror. It was a no-win situation. As a matter of fact, we hardly spoke the rest of the trip. I did most of the driving, and Junior did the navigating. Each of us had our own abilities, which is one of the things Junior could never understand.

"Everyone," he would proclaim, "should be equal in the ability department."

The second night on the road, we camped at a rest stop along the interstate about forty miles north of Laredo. While sharing small talk about the next day's leg of the journey, much-needed sleep slowly overcame both of us. Sounds of insects and other night creatures had an eerily soothing effect on us weary travelers.

The next morning, we woke to warm red sunlight streaming through the windshield. Another beautiful day, and a new day often gives you a fresh perspective on things. Junior was surprisingly agreeable. Our morning constitutionals completed, leftover potato chips and Twinkies washed down with lemonade, we were on the road once again.

As we entered Laredo, signs for the international border began looming along I-35. It wouldn't be long, now. Anticipation was mounting. The 'Mexico or bust' mentality was becoming a reality. It had taken roughly two-and-a-half days to drive the fifteen hundred miles to the border, and neither I, Junior, nor the old truck was worse for the wear. We made it in pretty fair shape--at least this far.

Once we crossed the border into Mexico, I figured it would be an additional eight hours to our final destination--Galeana, a small agricultural community nestled in the foothills of the Sierra Madre Orientals, about two hours south of Monterrey, and another two hours or so off the Pan American Highway. Following the signs on the bridge over the Rio Grande, I eased into the lanes designated for trucks and vans. Not much traffic for early morning. I wheeled the truck up to the customs both, just across the border in Nuevo Laredo, confident that our papers were in order this time.

Appearing to be a couple of suspicious characters to the man in the booth, he instructed us to pull ahead to a parking place. We dismounted, and Junior went around to open the double back doors for inspection. The false floor we had installed to hold valuables and supplies, may appear at first glance to be a perfect hiding place for contraband. However, it was criss-crossed with two-by-fours with a four foot square usable compartment in the middle. I designed that way in order to make better use of the space by building the floor up over the wheel wells inside the back end of the truck. The only access was gained by lifting up the carpet flap covering a two-by-four inside the back doors, and prying the board out with a knife or a screwdriver. Pretty ingenious.

The border guard appeared around the corner to perform his inspection. He was a middle-aged Latino wearing one-way dark glasses, and sporting a two day growth of stubble on his face. His gray customs uniform was neatly pressed, and his boots were highly shined---both signs that he was proud of his job and took it very seriously. The .357 Magnum resting in its black leather holster helped confirm that.

The guard walked slowly around the truck, giving both it and the two of us a quick, but thorough and silent examination. He came around to the back, looking through the open double doors, first at the interior of the truck with all its living room comfort, then at the trapdoor at the end of the false floor.

"Open it," was all he said.

"Yes sir," I complied, grabbing the screwdriver Junior had lain right inside the back door and prying the board loose, revealing neat rows of canned goods on one side, tools and spare parts on the other side.

"Where are you going?" the guard inquired in a thick accent, nodding his approval.

"To a village in the mountains south of Monterrey," Junior offered a bit nervously. "Galeana."

"En los montanas? Aha, communistos!" the guard almost laughed out loud, pleased with himself that we silly gringo boys were possibly headed for trouble.

"Communists?" Junior tried to grasp the relevance of the guard's remark.

"Quiet, I'll tell you later," I cautioned under my breath.

"Okay, my young friends, you may go now," The guard said, walking away and chuckling to himself. "But be careful of the communistos."

"What the hell was he talking about?" Junior turned to me with a terrified look on his face.

"I did a little homework on the area all around Monterrey," I replied. "It seems Communism is pretty widespread in certain third world countries. Its influence is strong on the poor, less-educated people like the ones we'll be working with. I read in Time Magazine where there are a lot of small groups trying to work the mountain villages between Monterrey and Mexico City. Back in the day, Mexican revolutionaries such as Pancho Villa and Emiliano Zapata worked to overthrow conservative governments, becoming folk heroes in the process. Later, along come Fidel Castro from Cuba, and Che Guevara from Bolivia, both in the business of liberating poverty-stricken populations from dictatorships throughout Central and South America. Of course, Castro had close ties with the Soviet Union. One of the Communist ideals he wanted the poor people of rural areas of Mexico was distribution of wealth. We'll probably see posters of these guys in Galeana. So, that's sort of it in a nutshell."

"Really?" Junior asked with a hint of dismay. "Do you think any of these guys are in Galeana?"

"Probably, but don't worry about it. We're not going there to rid the world of Communism." I really had no idea, but Junior was buying every bit of it.

With the first real words exchanged between us for two days, we climbed back into the truck and wound our way through the busy streets of Nuevo Laredo, following the signs to the Pan American highway, and to Monterrey.

Once we were on the main highway headed south, I kicked back and relaxed a bit behind the wheel. Junior, surprisingly enough, did the same. He began to make positive comments about the desert terrain, and the beautiful weather we'd experienced so far on the trip. He even spoke of the widespread communism down here being so much hogwash. Actually, there was some truth to what the boarder guard had said, but he'd kind of spiced it up a bit for our benefit. Plus, I sort of fed Junior a line just to watch him get all worked up.

Monterrey at rush hour. What a numbing experience! I swore that if we made it through this city unscathed, I would possess the ability to drive any type of vehicle anywhere in the world. The main four-lane leading into the north edge of the city had unexpectedly narrowed down to two lanes. Kamikaze taxi drivers in their garish cabs wove in and out of traffic, passing cars and trucks at breakneck speeds. Heavily laden trucks and buses packed with commuters competed for the lead in a single-file race to whatever destination. I just held on, white-knuckling it and hoping someone would win the race and traffic would begin to thin out. Where the hell are people going that they have to drive so fast, and what do they do when they get there? There must have been something about that space behind the wheel that consumes people with a competitive spirit. Gladiators of the road.

Monterrey was the heart of a highly industrialized area of Mexico, and we unknowingly picked a market day to pass through the city. Nearing the southern outskirts, traffic once again resumed its normal speed and distance. The bumper-to-bumper race to the winner's circle had subsided to no more than a pleasant drive in the country.

The Sierra Madre foothills loomed in the distance, forming a jagged horizon to the southwest. The heat and humidity of Monterrey, that clung like a hot towel, gave way to the cooler, crisp air of the highlands. The old truck seemed to be working a little harder to maintain highway sped. Appearing to be driving down a long, steady grade, we were actually driving uphill. The illusion was fascinating.

The hills became steeper by the mile, and the highway began to meander through them like a great snake. Heavy trucks hauling produce, livestock, and an unseen assortment of cargo, ground their way through the steep labyrinth at a snail's pace. The sweet stench of butane, a fuel cheaper than diesel, hung heavily in the thinning air. Some truck drivers had propped open their hoods with pieces of wood to prevent their straining engines from overheating.

It was rather unusual that all the trucks I'd seen on the road south of Monterrey had huge iron grates on the front. They appeared to be a type of insurance. Occasionally, a wild burro would wander down out of the foothills making a suicidal attempt to cross the highway in search of water. The only testimony given to these unfortunate animals was a rotting carcass or skeletal remains lying by the roadside bleaching in the sun. The huge trucks with the *cowcatchers* bolted on the front, were reminiscent of trains in the old west. They would always emerge victorious over animals straying into their paths. And, undamaged. What really amazed and angered me was the indifference the Mexicans held toward this highway slaughter.

There was about three hours of daylight remaining as we passed through Saltillo and Montemorelos, both small agricultural centers several miles off the Pan American Highway. With roughly forty miles to the end of our journey, all the planning, anticipation, and the rigors of the trip itself had shown through like a beacon in the night. We had done it. Our odyssey was nearly complete. The *Friends* signs emblazoned on the truck sides would attest to the work that lay ahead in the coming months.

We rolled into Galeana around seven that evening. It was a small town of maybe fifteen-hundred, mostly farmers or shop keepers. Block buildings painted with an assortment of pastel colors and intermingled with adobe houses lined with graveled streets. The sweet aroma of peppers and other spices, and bread baking permeated our senses. Our spirits soared as I eased the truck through the narrow streets. A small group of children playing stick-ball in the street stared at the lumbering white behemoth in utter amazement as I stopped and asked them for directions to the church, our home for the summer.

"Buenos Dias," I said in my best Spanish. "Donde esta la iglesia Protestante?"

The kids must have gotten a kick out of the gringo trying to speak their language, or the funny-looking truck, because they all giggled, pointing toward the church, about half a block down the street on the left. It was an unfinished cinder block building with gaping openings instead of windows, just as the missions council had described.

5. The Summer of '69

Our 'home on wheels' rocked to a halt in front of the uncompleted Protestant church. Our mission completed, but exhausted from the grueling drive up through the mountains, Junior and I jumped down from the truck onto the graveled street to stretch our legs. I didn't know how he missed it, but I landed dead square in the middle of a pile of horse manure with both feet. That short, but comical performance brought tears of laughter to our eyes.

"Road apple alert!" Junior whooped, thoroughly enjoying the moment.

Scraping the horse crap off my shoes with a stick, I looked around, noticing how peaceful the setting was in that small town. The jagged foothills of the Sierra Madre Occidentals protected the peaceful village to the south and east. The setting sun cast a warm golden glow on the western face of the hills. Scattered stands of cactus and scrub pine dotted the hillsides, even cropping up in the empty spaces between buildings. If not for the more modern buildings mixed with adobe houses, you might feel as if you were being swept back in time to somewhere in the old west.

A couple of doors down from where Junior and I were standing was a small gas station with a single pump out front, and a primitive, but practical lean-to garage on the far side. Stacks of old used tires and worn out engine parts indicated that the owner had a pretty good trade established. Next door to the station was a local watering hole. A few dilapidated cars and pickups sat on the street out front. Laughter and salsa music emanated from within the saloon doors.

"Good location for a bar," I commented to Junior, who was busy taking in his surroundings. "Just down from the church, or was it the other way around?"

The Protestant church was one of the more modern buildings in this mountain village. Blending in quite well with its surroundings, it was a plain two story cinderblock structure of the same primitive construction as all the others, with two exceptions: the small wooden spire placed on the peak of the roof in front, and the twin staircases cascading in opposite directions down the front of the church from the main entrance on the second floor to meet in a narrow court yard below. One day, when it was finished, the church would be a beautiful monument to the missionaries.

A stocky, middle-aged man with black wavy hair and graying temples approached from the alley alongside the church. Dressed in a yellow polo shirt and faded blue jeans, his rugged outdoor look was further defined by the dusty pair of cowboy boots on his feet.

"Hi, Brother Jorge Rivera," he greeted us each with a vigorous handshake and a smile a dentist would have been proud of. "Welcome to Galeana. Glad to meet you guys. We heard you were coming, but weren't exactly sure when you'd arrive. Folks at your church said to be on the lookout for a big white van, so this must be it," he said, gesturing toward the truck.

"So, how was the trip?" he asked with genuine interest.

"We had a little trouble getting out of Iowa," I replied. "But after that everything went pretty smooth." Glancing at Junior, I gave him a *don't say it* look.

"Well, glad you made it okay. You go ahead and park your truck out back of the church," Brother Jorge said, pointing to the narrow alley next to the church. "When you get situated, come on in the back door and meet the gang." Jorge lead the way to insure all the local kids that started gathering to stare at the truck were out of the way. The children played wherever they could find room.

Driving that big truck down that narrow alley was like trying to pilot a loaded barge down the Mississippi between two sandbars during dry season. The going was painfully slow, and it took Junior and me watching both sides to guide it through. The right front wheel went up over a rock, causing the old girl to sway, scraping the second floor overhang of the building. Losing a little white paint to the rough cement, we finally made it through. I maneuvered the old truck around the small lot behind the church, backing it into an out of the way corner.

A small group of people in the basement of the church were just finishing up their evening meal when Junior and I walked in. Jorge graciously introduced us to everyone. There were about a dozen teenagers and two adult leaders from a large church in St. Paul, Minnesota, plus a small group from Detroit. There was also the local Baptist minister, Brother Isidro, a balding man in his late fifties. His young wife, a very shy woman in her early twenties, appeared to be nearly nine months pregnant. The two made rather an odd couple, and neither spoke English.

Lastly, Jorge introduced his nephew, Carlos Olivo, a former factory worker from Downey, California, and his wife Susie. Carlos seemed pleasant enough, but somewhat reserved, while Susie was the polar opposite. She began to recite scripture right away to us, lecturing us about our spiritual and financial obligations while doing mission work.

Susie further pointed out that we would have to scrap our plans for sleeping in the truck, and move into a local hotel room she had assigned us to, as well as pay our summer fees up front. Junior and I were well aware that it would cost us each two hundred and fifty dollars for the summer, but we didn't think we'd get hit between the eyes with it the minute we walked in. No problem, I thought. Just play the game, do what we're told, and maybe we'll see a good side to all this.

"I'll bet you guys are hungry after such a long trip," Jorge offered with a smile, trying to melt some of the ice Susie had left us with. "There's plenty left, grab a plate and help yourselves. Later on, Carlos can run you over to the hotel and get you settled in."

Jorge shooed us over to the buffet table where the remnants of a genuine home-cooked meal was waiting to be finished off. Hot stew, fresh rolls, and ice cold lemonade sure hit the spot after three days of junk food. As we dined, muffled conversations continued around the large basement dining room. Noticing Susie and Carlos talking to the youth group from St Paul, I gently nudged Junior's knee under the table to get his attention.

"Where'd she come from? I asked under my breath, nodding in Susie's direction.

"You know who wears the pants in that family." Junior nearly choked on a mouthful of bread, trying to keep from laughing out loud.

When we finished eating the sumptuous dinner, Jorge and Carlos came over and sat down at our table. Jorge handed me a mimeographed itinerary, not unlike a sort of training schedule, listing everything the group did in a seven day week. Each day began with calisthenics at six-thirty. Breakfast was promptly at seven-fifteen, followed by morning worship and bible study from eight until nine-thirty. Then, off to one of the outlying villages to visit the sick and elderly, passing out religious pamphlets written in Spanish. Later on in the week, another visit was scheduled to the same village to hold evening services. Sort of like a farmer tending his crops, or a shepherd tending his flock.

Jorge further explained to us that Susie and Carlos were the administrators of the Friends church, and the group had financial obligations to meet which called for the prompt payment of summer tuition. Since it was explained to us in that way, we had no problem with it.

With all the amenities and administrative details out of the way, Carlos offered to walk us over to the hotel and help us get checked in. Since Spanish was his first language, his offer was gratefully accepted.

The walk to the hotel was a short three blocks from the church. The evening sun had set, leaving behind a bright pink and purple sky. Old-style incandescent street lights began to come on, illuminating the shadowy street corners. Small pockets of towns-people were enjoying a stroll in the cool evening air. Periodically, Carlos would stop and greet folks in their native language. Junior and I didn't understand a lot of the exchanges, but the idea was clear. Mostly, we just smiled and nodded.

The front of our hotel was a storefront divided by a narrow walkway leading into a central courtyard. Potted cactus roses lined the courtyard beneath the ground floor windows. Between the second floor balconies, pulley clotheslines were strung bearing the day's laundry. An overhanging tin roof protected each doorway from sudden downpours. Patched and painted a blinding turquoise, although very neat and clean, the courtyard resembled a scene from a Bogart movie.

The owner of the hotel, a short, plump woman with distinctive Indian features and a waist-length cascade of black hair, came out of one of the rooms, greeting Carlos like an old friend. They stood in the dimly lit courtyard, talking and laughing in a mixture of Spanish and local dialect. I surmised it was important for the people at the church to have a good rapport with the townspeople.

Carlos introduced us to the woman, in Spanish of course.

"Much gusto," we both replied, remembering the crash course in Spanish we'd taken at the church in Marshalltown. With that, she led the way to our room.

A small double, the room was filled with mismatched furniture. The walls were painted the same bright turquoise as the rest of the hotel. The bedding on the twin beds clashed violently with the color of the walls. Interior design and color taste was definitely not foremost in the minds of the hotel owners, but the room was spotless, as well as cozy. This would be our home for the summer. I had to admit it seemed far more inviting than sleeping on the floor of that truck every night.

In broken phrases of gringo Spanish, we thanked the hotel owner for everything, as she turned to leave the small room. Carlos bid us a good evening, reminding us to be at the church promptly at seven-fifteen for breakfast. On our first day, he would allow us to skip calisthenics. That was awful nice of him, I thought to myself. I just hoped that Susie would approve. Carlos waved back at us as he descended the stairs, following the Indian woman to the office.

"Home, sweet home," Junior muttered with a tone of sarcasm as he unpacked his bags.

"Hey, it's not so bad. Who knows, we might even learn to enjoy it. Maybe spend the rest of our lives here."

"Not this kid."

"Why, Junior, are you homesick already?" I teased.

"It's not that," he whined. "All this is going to take some getting used to, that's all."

Sensing he was really serious, I changed the subject by offering to take the bed in the corner, so he could have the one by the window.

"No, you go ahead and take the window bed, since you smoke."

"Thanks, don't mind if I do." Junior's offer was totally out of character.

Stretching out for a much-needed night's rest, I gazed out the window at the stars twinkling in the black velvet sky. A half-moon cast an eerie contrast of shadows and moon-light in the courtyard below. Visions of Junior leaving for home entered and exited my thoughts, as sleep slowly tightened its grip on me.

I was awakened by the obnoxious clanging of my alarm clock at six-thirty of our first day in Galeana. Crawling out of bed and splashing cold water in my face from the earthenware pitcher on the dresser, I noticed Junior was still fast asleep. I called his name. No response. I shook his foot. Still no response. *Is it alive? Let's check!* Standing next to his bed, I leaned over, compressing the mattress into the springs with all my strength, then releasing it. The whole bed bounced on the old springs like a big car with worn-out shock absorbers. *Aha! It is alive!*

"Mmmph, quit." Junior moaned his displeasure at being so rudely snatched from the arms of slumber.

"Let's go. Time to get up. Got about twenty minutes to get to the church."

"But it's still dark out, " mumbled the living dead.

"No it's not. Look out the window. I guess when you're face down in your pillow, everything looks dark."

"What did I get myself into?" Junior moaned.

"Come on, be a man," I teased. Junior was slowly coming to a boil with my teasing, but he was like that every morning.

The sweet smell of a hearty breakfast being cooked greeted us as we entered the back door of the church. The dining room was alive with conversation when we took our place in the serving line. Some of the kids from the St Paul group came over and introduced themselves, telling us how good it was that we could share in helping to spread the Word.

One person standing in the breakfast line sort of stood out from the rest. She was a couple people ahead of me, so I stepped up beside her so it didn't look like I was crowding in line, and introduced myself. She smiled and introduced herself as Marlo Anderson, one of the adult leaders from Detroit. Marlo was short and petite with an hour-glass figure and spoke with a deep sultry voice. Her shoulder length hair framed her well-tanned face like a halo. The way she enunciated certain words told me she was a singer. Under normal circumstances, I was never at a loss for words, but in the presence of such radiance, all I could do was smile at her.

I glanced around, up and down the line at the other kids, catching the eye of a guy who must have seen me talking to Marlo. He returned my glance with a sort of sideways smirk, glanced at Marlo, then back at me, smiling. He was twitching his eyebrows and again with that smirk as if to say, "Yeah, she's looking for another notch on her gun. Be careful." I didn't think much about it at the time, but later on, my life was to be deeply affected by my relationship with Marlo.

Tapping a spoon on his water glass to get everyone's attention, Brother Jorge announced himself at the head of the table.

"Go ahead and finish eating, everyone," he called out. "I just wanted to remind all of you that we'll be going to El Verde to hold children's bible school this morning. Now, it's quite a ways out from where we can park the vans, so you may want to hurry and get on some good walking shoes before we head out. Everyone be back here in twenty minutes. Praise the Lord!"

"Praise the Lord!" everyone replied in unison. That was a daily ritual we would soon get used to. That was Friends' way of asking everyone, *"Are you happy?"* They would answer, *"Yes, we're happy!"*

The entire group met at the vans in back of the church in record time. All the guys were dressed casually in jeans, T-shirts, and hiking boots.

All the girls were wearing dresses or skirts and blouses, with tennis shoes. Local customs prevented women from wearing jeans, T-shirts, or shorts.

El Verde was a small farming village on a lush plateau on the far side of a deep gorge. We parked the vans in a clearing on the side of the dirt road next to a narrow foot bridge. Jorge was right. It was quite a ways off.

Crossing the foot bridge was not for the faint of heart. Looking down made one dizzy from the height. Dropping a stone off the bridge, I counted the seconds until I saw it splash in the tiny stream below. About ten to twelve seconds. No sound. Just a microscopic ripple in the stream.

The rest of the group had crossed the bridge, as I stood in the warm morning sunlight looking at the tiny stream far below. Marlo came up beside me to see what I was doing. The fragrance of her hair permeated my senses.

"Wouldn't you just love to climb down there, take off all your clothes, and lie in the sun?" she cooed suggestively.

"Uh, me, us, …now? I stammered. As ludicrous as her invitation sounded, it was not without merit.

"Come on, you know we can't, " she laughed. "I was just kidding."

Teasing would have been a better word. Marlo tossed her hair back and did the model-on- the-runway walk to the far side of the bridge. Realizing how totally absurd her suggestion was, I shrugged it off and continued across the footbridge.

At the end of the bridge, a slight incline led up to the meadow below the village . Some of the children saw us coming and ran down the dirt path to greet us. They were so cute; so eager to run down the path and lead everyone back to the village. None of the kids were wearing shoes, and every nose needed wiping. Typical kids, I thought, but the clothes these kids were wearing were most likely some of the very few they owned.

This area of Mexico was very depressed economically. The men of the village were truck drivers, farm hands, or common laborers. Minimum wage was something the United States dreamed up, not Mexico. There was something very special about these people, however. What little they did possess, they were more than willing to share with other people. Also, they appeared to be happy, well adjusted, and highly principled folks.

The Friends had obviously visited El Verde several times in the past. Two village elders came out of an adobe house to greet our group. Carlos and Jorge shook hands, exchanging embraces with the two older men, then turned and introduced Junior and I as the newest members of Friends.

The group walked from one adobe home to the next, speaking with just about everyone in the small village and inviting them all to the local church for a sing-along and a short morning service. We never set a time for these gatherings; they could just join in when they arrived.

That particular morning, the small one-room adobe chapel was filled to capacity. Folks were even standing outside, listening and peering through the open windows. One of the village elders handed Marlo a battered flattop guitar and a bar stool. She sat down, expertly testing the chords on the old instrument, then began singing *How Great Thow Art*, first in Spanish, then English. It was beautiful. Her voice was that of an angel.

Heightened by Marlo's singing, the spiritual mood in the tiny chapel began to reach a fever pitch. More hymns were sung in Spanish, and testimonies were given by anyone who felt moved to stand and tell his or her story. Either Carlos or Jorge would interpret for the members of our group. Emotions ran unihibited in the small church. Tears flowed like tiny rivers. People lifted their hands high in the air, praising God and embracing each other.

At the end of the service, Jorge dismissed the crowd with a powerful prayer and benediction, bringing more cries of praise and acknowledgement from the congregation. Winding down from the emotional crescendo he was riding, he announced to the youth group that lunch had been prepared by some of the women of the village, and encouraged us all to mingle and talk with the good people of El Verde.

After a delicious meal of goat stew, flour tortillas, and cinnamon tea, we headed back across the bridge to the vans, bidding a fond 'via con Dios' to the people of El Verde. I was still amazed by the fact that, as poor as these people were, they insisted on treating outsiders like royalty. No reflection on my mom, but I didn't eat that well at home! Giving to others was a pleasure these people truly enjoyed, If the whole world felt that way, I thought, there would be no wars, no hate, and no famine.

The weeks passed like a whirlwind from one to the next. Each day brought a new adventure. Marlo and I would always try to steal a quiet moment in some out of the way place, to talk and get to know each other better. Occasionally, we would end up in a passionate embrace. Afterwards, however, I would feel a deep sense of frustration, and of being used. I sensed that Marlo was using her sexuality to manipulate and control me. As time passed, being with her was like an addiction.

With each passing day, I tried hard to understand what our relationship was all about. Marlo became increasingly possessive and domineering each time we were together. In my confused state, I tried to focus on the true reasons I came to Mexico, and began looking forward to traveling to the next village and attending the next service.

Each village we visited held a different enchantment and a whole new set of emotional and spiritual experiences all its own. Each night of the week, we'd hold services in a different town. We'd pack up the projector, screen, and a small Honda generator and show a film in Spanish. Sometimes the little kids were more intrigued with all the equipment than with the movie.

The frustration I felt about my relationship with Marlo was leading to a reconsideration of its effect on me. I was growing tired of having to justify my every word, act, or deed, to say nothing of being sexually teased constantly.

By the middle of August, there came an opportunity to travel by pack burro to the village of Diez Y Ocho. Literally translated, meaning Eighteen, the small village backed up to the foothills, and was the last of a string of eighteen villages along an arroyo that doubled as a road during the dry season. The road was inaccessible during the rainy season, which normally began around the first of October. That date, however, didn't preclude the possibility of a sudden cloudburst. The inherent danger that lay with the unpredictable rain at times turning the dry river bed into a raging torrent, together with a trip by burro prompted Jorge to make the trip strictly voluntary. I quickly signed up to go.

That decision was met by opposition on two sides. First of all, Marlo refused to understand why I chose to go. Of course, I found her very attractive, but by this time I was disenchanted and fed up by her possessive, narcissistic behavior.

"I'll see you in a few days," I simply said, not being very tolerant of such treatment from her or anyone else.

"Gary," she blurted out, "if you go up there, we're done!"

"Fine," I said, turning and walking away.

That really made her mad. We hardly spoke the rest of the summer. The other problem with my decision to make the trip was Junior. He'd gotten homesick to the point of wanting to just pack up and go home. We discussed it in the hotel room while I packed a few things for the trip to Diez Y Ocho.

"I'm just tired of the whole deal here!" he whined. I'm still trying to get over my first case of Montezuma's revenge! I hate the hours we keep! And besides, I miss Lynda."

"Who the hell is Lynda?"

"Oh, that's right, you never met her, did you? She's a girl I met at band practice. I told her I'd probably be gone only a month. Well, the month's long passed, so I'm leaving."

"Okay, fine." By this time, I'd had it with his constant whining and bad attitude anyway.

"Tell you what, take the truck, park it in my back yard and let my folks know what's going on. Then, we'll settle up when I get back home. You're not going alone are you? It's a long trip."

"No, one of the guys from Detroit wants to go back, too. I'm dropping him off in Des Moines, then he'll take a bus the rest of the way."

"We're leaving for Diez Y Ocho this afternoon, so I guess this is it, huh?"

"Yeah, we'd better leave this morning. Get a good start. We could probably get as far as Laredo by tonight."

"Well, good luck and have a safe trip." I meant that more for the truck's sake than Junior's. I hated to see him go, although he really hasn't been happy since we arrived in Galeana.

Our group had been gone from the church in Galeana for four days. The trip to Diez Y Ocho had been a success. Every evening, we held revival meetings in the mountain village. People had come from neighboring communities along the arroyo to share in the singing and soul-saving. Members of the Friends had hearts filled with joy just being a part of it. I was glad to be back for one reason--I couldn't have taken much more of that burro saddle!

Jorge, however, measured the terms of success of those camp meetings by the number of souls saved. He became increasingly obsessed with numbers. Quantity, rather than quality. That obsession crept into every conversation he had with us.

"More, more!" he'd bellow. "We're not working hard enough!" After that outburst, however, it was agreed that we all needed to cut back a little. We'd been holding services twice a day, seven days a week, plus visitation and anything else we could squeeze in for the past five weeks or so. We needed a break. The toll was showing on us all.

The rest of the summer's work was a collage of memorable experiences and near-tragedies. However good or bad, they all left a lasting impression on me. The Friends had spent a week in Monterrey holding revival meetings at a large Baptist church. Everyone received their share of blessings that week. This time, however, we recognized the need for a break now and then, so we took every opportunity to go sight seeing.

One day, a bunch of us decided to have our hair styled at one of the high dollar unisex salons. Since I only spent twenty dollars having my hair coiffed, I thought it would be cool to buy some new clothes and a pair of sunglasses. Boy, I looked like Tony Montana in my new sharkskin slacks, cotton shirt, and gangster sunglasses! The day had been exceptionally hot, so we all met at the University of Monterrey swimming pool. So much for the hair styles.

On the trip back to Galeana, I was given the task of driving the camper for Brother Isidro, his wife, and their three kids. Their new baby was born last month, and they had with them their little boy, five years old, and their daughter about six. Isidro and his wife, with the baby on her lap, were in the cab of the ancient International pickup with me, and the two little kids were in the back of the camper on a mattress.

I'd picked up our weekly ration of six gallon glass bottles of water at a warehouse on the way out of town, and headed south on the Pan American highway. Everything was good. The weather was balmy, the old truck was running smoothly, even at seventy miles an hour.

Suddenly, without warning, the hood came unlatched and flew up, smashing against the windshield and blocking my view of the road ahead. The old pickup careened from one side of the two lane highway to the next. Amidst the fearful prayers of Isidro, the blood-curdling screams of his wife, and the frantic cries of the baby, I heard and felt the right front tire explode, followed by the sickening side-to-side lurch of the truck spinning out of control.

Sliding to a dusty halt, backwards in a shallow ditch on the opposite side of the highway, I sat frozen behind the wheel for several seconds with my face buried in my hands, thankful to be alive. I looked over at Isidro and his wife and the baby. They were holding each other tightly, crying and praising God for their deliverance from death. Isidro looked up at me with terror in his eyes.

"Oh, my God!" I yelled, kicking the door open and running to the back of the camper. Throwing open the tailgate, the three of us peered in and saw two small, wide-eyed children, sitting in the far corner, clutching each other amidst shards of broken glass. They were both drenched with the water from broken bottles, but miraculously, neither had a scratch on them. Cautiously, I extricated the kids from their razor-sharp trap, handing them out to their parents' waiting arms. We all stood in the ditch alongside the highway, embracing, all very thankful to be alive.

With the tire changed and the battered hood wired securely in place, the five of us and the baby crowded into the cab of the truck. I eased back out onto the highway, heading towards Galeana. To break the tension, we sang Spanish hymns all the way back to the church. Songs that make you smile and clap your hands.

Exhausted from the trip and near fatal accident, we pulled into the lot behind the church. A couple of guys from Michigan who had stayed behind came out to greet us. Noticing the caved-in hood and shattered windshield, they both gave me a shocked look.

"What the...what on earth happened? Were you guys in an accident?" Roy Clayton asked. Roy was a stout farm boy from a small town near Detroit. Slow-witted, but with a quick temper.

"The hood flew up, then I blew a tire. The only thing hurt, besides my pride, was a couple bottles of water in the back."

"My bible!" he cried, running to the back of the camper. "I paid twenty-five dollars for this! Now look at it!" he howled, holding up the dripping, leather-bound bible. The rich leather binding had been scarred by the broken glass, and the gilded pages were a soggy, tattered mess.

"Sorry about your bible, pal," I said with a mixture of anger and embarrassment in my voice.

"Come here, let me show you something," I said sternly, taking Roy by the shirt sleeve and leading him to where Isidro's son and daughter were playing. "See these two little kids? You take a good long look at them, and thank God they're even alive. They were in the back of the truck when this happened. Now look at me and tell me you think more of your precious bible than you do of these kids!" By then, I was furious, and he knew it. Roy wouldn't even look me in the eye. All he did was grit his teeth, looking at his ruined bible, then at the ground.

The suppressed doubts I had about this group and my own motivation for working in Galeana only intensified with time. First, it was Susie's little lecture my first day here, then Jorge melting down like he did, and finally, the water-logged bible. Besides that, my underwear kept mysteriously disappearing off the clothesline at the hotel, which was just wrong. Negative feelings were starting to imbue this whole thing. I began to wonder if I was even supposed to be here. I even doubted if there was really any divine intervention on the highway. The miracle I'd thought I witnessed now seemed no more than good driving skills.

I really needed a change. That change came in the form of the Friends' annual retreat to Mexico City and Acapulco. There would be plenty of relaxation time; we'd only hold a one-night meeting in each city.

Mexico City was beautiful in late August. The largest city in Mexico, it was situated in a highland basin known as the Valley of Mexico, and surrounded by mountains on three sides. Located at a higher elevation, Mexico city was cooler temperature-wise than what I was used to in Galeana. The cultural center of Mexico, the city was a lot to take in. The ancient Toltec ruins and the Pyramids of the Sun and Moon were highlights of our short stay.

With the merry-go-round crush of city traffic behind us (Mexico City had it's share of traffic rotundas), we headed south for Acapulco. The sun was beginning to set, yet I could see the gradual transformation of the landscape from mountainous plateaus to lush jungle wetlands near the Pacific coast.

Acapulco was a sort of fairytale place. White sandy beaches lines with swaying palms and crystal water reflecting the color of the sky made us feel we'd stumbled into paradise. Well, anyway, the next day was like that. When we arrived at around ten that night, it began to rain with a vengeance. Sort of like the old Sadie Thompson movie; a tropical paradise under water.

By the following morning, the rain had ended, and we spent three glorious days basking in the sun, forgetting all the tensions and doubts of the summer's work. I even contemplated more about the war in Vietnam, something that hadn't entered my mind since I left home.

The time had come to pack up once again and return to Galeana. Soothing trade winds, pina coladas secretly ordered from understanding beach waiters, and the death-defying cliff divers soon would be fond memories.

The youth group from the Baptist church in Marshalltown was waiting to greet us on our arrival at Friends' church in Galeana. My old friend Dave Hansen was among them. I was surprised to see him since he wasn't sure if he would be able to come.

"Hey, Bud, good to see you! Jesu Christo!" he jubilantly called out. That was about all the Spanish poor Dave could ever remember.

"Good to see you too, man. Hey, watch how you say that. These folks might think you're cussin' at 'em," I cautioned jokingly.

"Oops, sorry. Hey, that's a good looking beard you've got going there," he noted, testing the week-old stubble on my face. I'd decided to lose my razor for a while. Sort of a rebellion, I supposed.

The group from Marshalltown spent a week with us, going out to villages during the day and holding revivals in the evening. Little by little, my spiritual strength was returning. I felt more a part of the mission in Galeana once again, even regaining lost trust in certain members of the group.

Cliff Williams, one of the adult leaders in my home group, and one of the church leaders, came up to me one day with a startling revelation. He informed me that he had been in contact with my parents and that they'd asked him to bring me home with them.

"You owe it to your parents and the church to return with the group," he proclaimed.

"But, when I left home, I told Mom and Dad I'd be home when I walked through the door," I pleaded. "I thought I had their blessing." I wanted to argue further, but out of respect for Cliff, I didn't.

"They've evidently changed their minds," Cliff replied. "I think it's just best if you come back with us. We'll be leaving in a couple of days." He was pretty adamant about it. Typical, though. He usually got his way. Cliff Williams was president of a manufacturing company back home and one of the church's largest financial supporters.

Bags packed once again, addresses and promises to write each other exchanged, I bid a tearful and reluctant goodbye to the group I'd worked with so closely, lived with, and shared unbelievable experiences with so much over the past months. I had learned one thing from working with the Friends' church, that being in order to work as a missionary, you must give all of yourself. I just wasn't ready to make that commitment. I was ready to go back home.

Seeing Marlo standing off to the side all by herself, I slowly approached her. As I did, though, she turned her glance away.

"Goodbye, It's been nice knowing you," I offered. We had some good times, didn't we?" Without a word, she turned and walked into the back door of the church.

The trip back to Iowa was a long, quiet one for me. I did a lot of reflecting about the past few months. I had left home a boy, and returned a man, in more ways than one. Pondering what the future held in store for me, thoughts of enlisting in the army again raced through my mind, yet that decision was no closer than it was in the spring.

Finally arriving in Albion, Cliff dropped me off at my home. I really did miss it, but never admitted it. I unloaded my bags, thanked Cliff for the ride, and walked slowly up to the house as he drove away. Mom met me at the back door with a startled look on her face.

"I thought you weren't coming home until later in the fall," she said, giving me a 'Mom' hug. I stood head and shoulders above her, but that never deterred her from being a mother.

"Welcome home, Jody," she said quietly. I always hated it when she called me that. "It's good to have you back anyway."

"You mean you and Dad didn't tell them to bring me home? The picture was becoming clearer now.

"No, Honey, whatever gave you that idea?"

"Well, he...that lying...! All summer, I've been lied to, used, stolen from, and then damn near killed!" Tears of frustration streamed down my face as she put her arms around me. Not a word was spoken between us as we stood there on the back porch.

"Why don't you go on in and lie down and get some rest," she gently prodded, finally breaking the silence. "We can talk later when you feel better."

That next Sunday, I went to church by myself, just as before. I was invited to stand up and tell my story of the summer's work before the congregation. Having delivered short sermons to poor, but receptive audiences in Mexico, I stood and confidently faced the huge gathering. It was a strange, new feeling, but somehow I expected a much better response than I received as I began to tell the story of how mine and the lives of Isidro and his family were spared on the highway that day.

Glancing across the sea of expressionless faces, I had the epiphany there was a huge difference between speaking to these, my own people, and the peasants in a small adobe chapel in a remote village in Mexico. Mexican people were far more eager and receptive to the bible, hear about a total stranger's everyday experiences, or listening to talk about miracles. These folks were different. Their apathy was unnerving.

On the way out the big oak doors at the front of the church, I met Junior's father. "Why's everyone acting so cold?" I probed, hoping he wouldn't say what I thought he was about to. "No one acted that strange before we left."

"I believe it's the beard," he confided discreetly, as if not to let anyone hear him speak. "You may want to lose it."

The beard. I was being judged for the way I looked rather than who I'd become. There was a story to tell about my experiences, but the beard was an apparent roadblock. I imagined that not too many folks in this average sized central Iowa town were accepting of beards on young faces in the fall of '69. Too radical.

Not meaning all that much to me, the beard came off. Ironically, the folks at the church warmed back up a little at a time, becoming more interested in hearing of my experiences. The church board even awarded me a one-semester scholarship to Judson, a fine arts college in Elgin, Illinois, the church was connected with. That was part of the original agreement for Junior and I spending the summer in Mexico. However, he came back early. Junior turned it down to join the Navy band, but I accepted the offer. I thought maybe going back to college was what I needed.

I still had a problem with the way I felt about the people in the church being judgmental of others for the way they looked, rather than what was in their hearts. Because of that attitude, no matter where the fault laid, or who was more selfish, I would take no active part in church for years to come.

The freedom of having transportation of my own at Judson was going to be a problem. The big white van would have to be traded for a car. But, Junior and that guy from Michigan had nearly run the old truck into the ground on the hasty trip back home. A careless combination of anxiety to get home and driving it too hard left the truck a tired, battered heap in my back yard. Dents and scratches lined both sides of the body. The side mirror on the driver's side had been knocked off its mount somehow. A long streak of dried vomit garnished the right side of the truck. Junior had gotten sick on the road, stuck his head out the door, hung on, and let it fly.

It took me several days to get the old truck running right once more. What I'd found was not unlike mistreating an old horse. The oil level was dangerously low, the battery and radiator were both dry, and there was a serious problem with the electrical system. I reattached the side mirror, installed a new battery, did a pressure test on the radiator, then filled all the fluids up to a normal level. After several attempts, the engine still refused to crank. Frustrated and out of ideas, Dad and I towed the old step van up town to a local garage. They had it fixed and running good that next afternoon. Now, a little cleaning up, and the old girl would be ready for the used car lot, once more.

After exploring several car dealerships' white elephant lots, I found a car that would match both my needs and my bank account. Not exactly the car of my dreams, I traded the old girl for a '57 Ford two-door post. A good reason I bought the beige sedan that day was the fact that I've always wanted a car like that, plus the affable salesman settled on an even trade.

The old Ford ran pretty good, but it needed a lot of work, so I drove it to a garage owned by a friend of my dad's for a complete once over. When he was done with it, the Ford was tuned to perfection, and by my request, the rusted-out exhaust system was replaced by a set of dual Cherry Bombs. Boy, Dad hated those things!

Always looking for the good in everybody, and in life itself, I was ready for my next big adventure; the next stop on the road to maturity. I was very optimistic about going back to college. Perhaps too optimistic. Like Marie and her rose-colored glasses, sometimes I saw the world in a better light than it actually was.

6. Judson, Another Stop Along the Yellow Brick Road

A six-hour drive from home, the Judson College campus was nestled in a secluded, wooded valley creating a picturesque view from its entrance off the main highway. Early frosts had painted the trees with an explosion of yellows and golds. Red brick dormitories overlooked a small lake in the center of the valley. Tree-lined drives circled up through the hills surrounding the lake. White-washed columns fronting the red brick buildings lent a Victorian air to the small, peaceful campus. The clever, functional design of the campus created a serene setting for higher learning.

Finding my way to the administration building, I began the process of class registration. Still unsure of my academic goals, I signed up for some basic freshman core courses. English Literature, Sociology, and a couple of fill-in classes were about all my scholarship would allow. Art and mixed chorus sounded good, so I chose them to round out my schedule.

Picking up the required items for my classes at the college book store, I ran into an old acquaintance from back home. She was a year ahead of me in high school and had been a member of the church back in Marshalltown.

Kathy Simmons was the only daughter of a wealthy manufacturer in Marshalltown. Since childhood, she had been showered with material well-being by her parents. As she grew up, Kathy had become the focal point of hormonal outbursts by her so-called boyfriends.

In high school, the ever-popular Kathy was a cheerleader for the Marshalltown Bobcats' football and basketball teams, which made her fair game for all the jocks. Searching for the meaning of life and love in all the wrong places, Kathy became pregnant in her senior year. Her folks begged God's forgiveness, packing her up to live with relatives, ultimately giving the baby up for adoption.

Kathy was always very attractive and the envy of her circle of friends. Her short blonde hair was always arranged in a Dutch boy cut. Just the right touch of makeup accented her stern, but sensuous features. The total 'preppie' image she possessed constantly conveyed her suggestive nature.

"Hi, Kathy, I didn't know you were coming over here to school," I stated rather apprehensively, not knowing if she'd recognize me.

"Hi yourself," she replied. "My folks sort of decided for me. Sort of a crash course on how to be a good girl."

"Well, you think it'll work?" I kidded, not wanting it to sound like a come-on.

"You never know. What're you taking this semester?"

"English Lit, Sociology, and a couple of basketball player courses."

"Really? Who have you got for Lit and Soc?"

"Let me see," I said, digging out my schedule. "Ingram for Lit on Monday and Wednesday in the lecture hall, and Sterling for Soc somewhere in one of the dorm buildings on Tuesday, Thursday, and Friday.

"Guess what?" she giggled. "Me too. I guess we'll show this place what it's all about."

"Well, maybe we'll both have someone to lean on and get through this."

During our first few weeks at Judson, Kathy and I both set out in earnest to study hard and try to get our lives straight. The interest we both showed in our classes began to reflect positively in our grades and our own personal lives. We'd spend late evenings at the library collectively getting our minds ready for a test, or working together on a paper.

As time passed, my interest in Kathy never grew to anything stronger than a bond between siblings. We'd scrap like brother and sister. Periodically, I would wonder why it was limited to that type of relationship, though, because she was so attractive.

Our friendship was based on mutual respect. We both realized that anything more would never be possible. Kathy came right out and told me in the beginning, so there would be no mistake. Trying to make it successfully through the academic meat grinder meant there was no room for a life-complicating romance.

There did come a time, however, when we both decided we should loosen up a bit, and learn to take advantage of certain situations just to make life a bit more interesting. One of these circumstances was the twice-weekly chapel service every student was required to attend. These services were a lot like a high school assembly, but they included a short sermon and hymn singing. Then, there were announcements concerning sports events, pep rallies, and newly formed rules governing campus life. All in all, pretty boring stuff. One way a lot of students at Judson found to escape these forced vespers was to seek a more earthly pastime by cutting chapel to spend the morning watching the weirdoes at the O'Hare terminal in Chicago.

Kathy was a little less willing to walk on the wild side, so it took some convincing on my part.

"Come on, Kath," I pleaded. "Do you realize we haven't taken one single chapel cut yet this semester? Let's just get in the car and go. We really need to get out of here for a while."

"Okay," she agreed reluctantly, "I guess we can't get into too much trouble. I have to run up to my room for a minute, so meet me out in the parking lot in front of the girls' dorm.

"Gotcha."

Kathy gave me that same rebuking smile she did whenever I said or did something crazy. It was her way of saying, "If I don't look out for you, no one will."

I turned the ignition key of the Ford just as Kathy climbed in the front seat beside me. She winced as the dual Cherry Bombs roared in protest. The noise always bothered her, so I would tease her by revving the engine. That was a little game we'd play; she'd get mad, and I'd keep aggravating her until she'd slap my arm. Brother and sister stuff.

I eased the Ford out onto the access road leading to I-90, east into Chicago. The morning rush hour had ebbed to a trickle of cars and trucks. Over the rear speakers, the traffic reporter on WLS in Chicago gave the all clear for the major arteries through the city.

Our little *Pinocchio* adventure was a great way of escaping our ho-hum existence at Judson. But, the campus was also a place where adventuresome souls would dabble in the sins of man, such as smoking in the dorm rooms (strictly prohibited by college rules), or walking up the access road to the Holiday Inn for a morning coffee break. Not considered outcasts by the majority of the student body, we would run into thirty or forty other Judsonites at the coffee shop on any given day. That was a very popular and convenient hangout. Furthermore, I ventured to say we'd run into a few familiar faces from Judson at O'Hare.

The thrill of playing hooky heightened as we turned off the expressway, heading towards the short-term parking lot by the main departure terminal. Huge, gleaming jet liners rumbled skyward overhead, filled with travelers headed to far-off destinations.

As we entered the main terminal building, Kathy was immediately drawn to the rows of gift shops, so she treated herself to the age old female ritual of window shopping. Together we walked for a while looking at the displays.

After a short while, I decided I could only handle so much of that, so I scoped out a comfortable spot to sit and begin the 'weirdo watch'. Spotting some lounge chairs just down the huge crowded corridor, I told Kathy to meet me there in an hour or so. She departed on her quest, and I sank deep into the comfort of a lounge chair to begin the game.

A never-ending assortment of people passed through the busy terminal that morning. Businessmen dressed for success hurried past carrying briefcases. Unmistakable tourists with cameras strapped on their necks strolled past. Tambourine wielding Hare Krishna followers pestered passersby with persistent requests to donate to their cause. Servicemen in uniforms emblazoned with hallmarks of valor, hurried past lugging heavy duffle bags.

From where I was sitting, I had a great view of people coming down the escalator. One individual on the moving staircase really caught my eye, and imagination, that morning. That person had become the center of my watching game.

The young army officer glided down the escalator like Pegasus descending from the mountaintop. On his head sat a dark green beret bearing a silver crest with crossed bayonets. His steal blue eyes darted back and forth as if seeking out and unseen enemy. Muscles flexed and strained beneath the green tunic as he shifted the weight of his duffle bag, revealing a silver bar on each shoulder, and the most awesome collection of medals I'd ever seen.

Leaning forward in the chair, I tried to count the medals on his chest. Counting five rows of three plus one at the top in the middle, I fantasized how he'd earned each one. How many of the enemy had he wiped out snatching his buddies from the jaws of death?

As the young warrior got off the escalator and disappeared into the crowd, I sank back into the chair and closed my eyes, thinking what it would be like. What would...it...be...like?

Each day melted into the next in the savage jungle. The gripping heat was so deadly , it could turn a man's brain to scrambled eggs leaving him a screaming, quivering mass of jelly in just minutes. The constant banging in my head, the shrill buzzing of carnivorous flies and mosquitoes sounded almost like, '"Go ahead and die, you bastard, make it easy for us!" Each step I took in this living sewer drug me further and further into the choking abyss. I had an eerie feeling I was being watched, stalked. I tried to shake off the terror of my paranoia by rationalizing this fear I wore like a glove was part of my Special Forces training at Fort Benning, that part which taught me to become keenly aware of my surroundings, suspicious of every sound, every shadow. Slowly, methodically, I made a mental check of the surrounding area. All around me was a thick, tangled mass of vines. Off to my right about fifteen yards was a small clearing next to a stream. A stand of bamboo on the far side of the stream! If I could reach it undetected, I could follow the stream to civilization, if there was such thing in this fetid world I was trapped in. Once reaching friendly lines, I would hand over the secret documents I retrieved from the Viet Cong compound. It was only yesterday, but it seemed like an eternity ago. The very outcome of this bloody, undeclared war depended on the success of my mission. Possibly, the end of democracy as we know it.

I felt a chilling presence. Suddenly, I felt a numbing pressure gripping my right arm. "No! It's not supposed to end like this! Not here! Not now!" The pressure on my arm became stronger, I wanted to cry out...

"Hey, wake up. Gary, wake up! What are you yelling about? What isn't supposed to end like this?"

Through the fog in my brain, I opened one eye. Kathy was standing over me, trying to shake me back to consciousness. She glanced around, noticing a crowd had gathered to watch my performance. I could see she was quite embarrassed.

Standing up on wobbly legs, I wiped the remnants of sleep from my eyes, took Kathy by the arm and strode through the small crowd around us.

"Sorry folks, bad childhood," I explained, smiling, as they shook their heads in disbelief.

We giggled like a couple of second graders all the way to the front exit of the terminal. Once we were outside, Kathy stopped laughing and turned to me.

"What was going on in there?" she asked. "Oh, I get it. You were off on one of your little trips again, weren't you?" Kathy was genuinely concerned that I may have had a few screws loose, but she was trying very hard to keep a straight face. We'd talked a lot about the daydreams I found myself in. The obsession I had with joining the Army was beginning to show. The dreams were becoming more real. I resolved to think more objectively about my reasons for enlisting. I wasn't exactly John Wayne or Audie Murphy.

"Oh, nothing. Just another stupid dream," I replied. "I saw this guy in uniform, and must have dosed off thinking what it'd be like to be where he's been. Sure had a chest full of medals,"

"Yeah, where's that, Vietnam? You really want to do all that?"

"Been thinking a lot about it lately," I conceded.

Slowly, I began to understand my own feelings. I was certainly no hero. There wasn't any real direction in my life. What I really needed was some regimentation, and pick up a skill in the process.

Walking to the car amidst the roar of departing jets, Kathy turned to me as if to say something, but she didn't say anything. She probably thought it best just to leave it lay.

We didn't talk much on the drive back to Judson that crisp November afternoon. The rumble of the Ford's unrestricted engine saw to that. At times, I felt a little self-conscious about the noise, but that afternoon, I welcomed the distraction.

The autumn afternoon sun was low on the horizon when we pulled into the parking lot by the girls' dorm. Announcing our arrival, I shook the serenity of the campus with a final blast from the Ford's dual pipes. That earned me a look of condemnation and a stinging slap on the arm from Kathy.

"Some people just never grow up, do they? she admonished with a grin. "I'll see you at supper. I'm going up to my room for awhile."

"Okay, I'll probably be in the student lounge."

"Don't forget, you need to get that report done for Sterling," she reminded. "It's due in a couple days."

"Yeah, yeah, I know. All I have to do is get my notes together and write it up." Actually, I'd forgotten all about that paper until she mentioned it, I hated to admit it, but I totally forgot what it was supposed to be about.

Wow! Deja vue! Just like at MCC! Slowly, once again, I was losing interest in college. The boring drudgery of studying hard to make good grades and trying to decide what the real benefits were, jelled to form the big question---what the hell am I doing here?

After supper, I tried to fill the rest of the evening with some TV in the student lounge. The large room was crowded as always, but unusual for a Thursday night. On one side of the room were the campus 'Trekkies', faithful followers of Star Trek adventures, patiently waiting for the magic hour, seven o'clock. On the opposite side of the TV room, were members of Judson's soccer team. Like oil and water, situations like this usually escalated and got pretty rowdy after a while, so I found an empty chair and watched the football game on the big console TV.

The jocks watching the game became increasingly physical and emotionally involved with the play in progress on the screen. Cheers and moans from the group nearly drowned out the announcer's voice, which had reached a heightened pitch during the very close game between the Jets and the Packers.

"Blah blah snaps the ball to whatshisname! Whatshisname runs it all the way from the forty yard line. It's a touchdown! With less than three minutes to go in the fourth quarter, the Packers lead the Jets by..."

"Captain's Log, Star date 3116.4, Captain James T. Kirk. The Starship Enterprise has just completed an exhausting mission to the planet Zircon, when we received a distress signal from a Federation freighter. It had reported being under a vicious attack from Klingon fighters. We had no choice but to..."

"Hey, Frodo, turn it back to the game before I rip your head off!" threatened Paul Jones, one of Judson's star soccer players.

"Yeah, do it! Do it! Take his head off!" cheers of encouragement rose up from Paul's teammates.

Paul was a fellow to be reckoned with. Not too many guys got in his way. A sort of self-made leader, he stood only about five-six, but struck an awesome pose. An all-state wrestler from his high school, Paul was built like a bulldozer, with fists like sledgehammers and a personality to match.

Frodo, on the other hand, was the leader of the Trekkies. This small, unwashed group of campus freaks also called themselves the 'Hobbits', each taking their names from Tolkien's *Lord of the Rings* series. Frodo, of course, being the head Hobbit.

Frodo's real name was Ray Jenkins. He was the same height as Paul Jones, but only half his weight. His long blonde hair had not been washed in the semester I'd known him. This was a requirement to become a member of the Hobbits, even for the girls. Each of them ironically were afflicted by the same degree of acne. Frodo was a very frail person for his age of nineteen, and if someone walked up behind him and hollered "boo", he would die of cardiac failure on the spot.

"Did you hear what I said?" Paul reaffirmed his threat. "Turn it back to the game before I wear this place out with you!"

Frodo walked nonchalantly over to the big console TV, reaching for the channel selector in a half-hearted attempt to appease Paul and the rest of the jocks, but decided against the submissive move. Retrieving his hand, he turned in the direction of the soccer team.

"Up yours!" he shrieked in defiance, strolling out of the student lounge with the rest of the Trekkies obediently at his heals.

With the exception of Mr. Spok logicalizing something on the yet unchanged channel, the lounge was quiet enough to hear a pin drop. All eyes were on Paul and his group, waiting for some type of response to the humiliation Frodo had handed him. But, with a triumphant "Oorah!", Paul beat his chest several times, strutted across the crowded lounge, switching the channel back to the Packers game.

Like so many other Thursday nights at Judson, this one was no different. The jocks would be living some gladiator sport on TV in the student lounge. If the Trekkies were lucky enough to get there first, they would be decked out in all their tacky early '60's finery, shouting praises to Captain Kirk and the entire crew of the Enterprise, calling out each one by name and official title.

I almost felt sorry for Frodo and his flock of Trekkies. Their only crime against society was being so damned indifferent to the torment they constantly subjected themselves to. Tonight, though, Frodo stood up to be counted. However slight, he made his mark. Feeling proud of the little guy, a grin crept across my face.

The crowd of Packers fans, reminiscing the high points of the humiliating defeat of the Jets, noisily made their way out of the student lounge. Some would meet at The Golden Bear, a pancake house used by the jocks as a center for social uplift and cultural excitement, across the Illinois River in Elgin. Others would go off for a late night rendezvous with their girl friends. Those who wanted to remain more practical and reserved would file back to their dorm rooms to prepare themselves academically and spiritually for tomorrow's encounters.

The late news was beginning, so I elected to hang around to see what new developments had reared their ugly heads in the Vietnam War. The lounge was deserted, so the choice of the three major networks was all mine. Switching the channel to a Chicago station I was familiar with, the national news found Cronkite and Jennings updating the American public on the latest fighting, allied gains and losses, and what the latest opinion polls thought of Lyndon Johnson's popularity.

Each time I watched the news for a war update, my interest in college dwindled a little more. I was obsessed with joining the Army. I kept thinking my enlisting would make a difference. That night, I began doing some serious thinking. Christmas break was coming up in a few short weeks, and I'd decided that Judson could continue without me.

7. Decision Time

Around 4:30 in the afternoon on December 20th, I pulled up in front of my parent's house in Albion. It was a crisp, clear day with the only hint of winter was the remnants of the last snow fall; slush had melted and dried on the streets. I stood on the sidewalk in front of the house looking, remembering.

The yard I gazed across was filled with childhood memories. The old elm tree still cradled the primitive, but thoughtfully designed tree house my brother and I had built, complete with a pulley and rope to haul up an afternoon snack, a stack of comic books, or a simple treasure to hide away in one of the secret compartments. Lots of summer days and nights were spent in that old tree house. The only distraction was the gentle breeze blowing through the tree branches, and the frame of our little hideaway straining against the movement of the friendly old elm tree's limbs.

The vegetable garden, carefully laid out by Mom in the corner of our one-acre lot, was bordered along the north side by a row of lilac bushes, and along the west side by a row of now dormant rhubarb. The memories of this garden were more like bad dreams; it was job of my brother Dennis and I to make sure it was kept weed-free.

In back of the house stood a small two stall garage Dad and I had built from the lumber of an old house we tore down four years earlier. The roof sagged in the middle where we spliced the old beams together. I claimed one of the stalls not being used to house a car, and cleaned up a corner of it. There was a litter of kittens living in a big box in the corner, and I used to lay down on an old rug on the dirt floor, letting them crawl over me, purring and tussling with each other.

The winter sun was beginning to set, with the night chill close on its heels. The sound of Mom opening the kitchen door and the sweet smell of a dinner roast brought me back to reality.

"Are you coming in or stand out there and catch your death?" Mom always had control of us kids, one way or the other.

"I'll be along, Mom, " I called back to her. "Just standing out here looking around."

When she called me in, I was thinking of the time she used to make me wear those big buckle overshoes to school, but I'd always take them off, hiding them at the head of the alley and going on to school. On the way home that afternoon, I'd stop and put them back on. No one would be the wiser.

"Your dad will be home pretty soon," she smiled. "Did you have a good trip?"

"Not bad," I replied, nodding toward the Ford parked in the street, "but I'm hearing a lot of strange new noises."

"Well, what do you expect? It's almost an antique…like me," she smiled, gesturing to her gray hair.

Since Dad didn't talk a lot during family meals, the dinner table conversation that night was centered on my two younger sisters, Gayle and Lorre. The topic was high school and boys. It amazed me how much they'd changed from focusing on Barbie dolls and slumber parties to high school and dating.

The discussion about my quitting school to enlist was never brought up at the dinner table that night. The best solution for me at this point was to return to Judson, finish out the winter term then come home and break the news later.

The long trip back to Elgin afforded plenty of opportunity to put together a plan. I would need a fulltime job and a cheap place to live, save a little money, then go back home when the time was right. The first week of March seemed so far away. Judson ran a trimester schedule, and that marked the end of the winter term.

The holidays seemed to come and go with the rapidity of normal days. Once there was a time when the anticipation and the excitement of Christmas held a certain magic for me. Half the fun was wondering what Santa would bring us. The other half was looking forward to all the snow, and snow days away from school. But, I looked back on some hellacious Iowa winters. Can't say as I missed that part. Now, most of the magic seemed to be missing.

Back on campus, the Holiday spirit had dwindled to memories, along with my interest in studying. Somehow, I continued to hold my head above water until the end of February. Kathy and I continued to talk at length about my decision to quit school and join the Army. She was never crazy about the idea of Vietnam and everything, but she respected my wishes.

Amazingly, I passed all my finals for the winter term. I'd made it, but the fact remained that college is not where I belonged. Not now. Saying goodbye to a few close friends and my teachers, I moved out of the dorm. It was a sad occasion, but I assured myself bigger and better things were in store.

Independence was not at all what I expected. The only marketable skill I possessed for potential employment was my own ambition. What I found was a job as a pump jockey at an all-night gas station in West Dundee, just across the interstate from the Judson campus.

My earnings from the gas station limited me to a tiny studio apartment for twelve dollars a week in Elgin. I shared a community bathroom with a retired truck driver and a guy that liked to drink a lot. It wasn't a whole lot of fun, especially when the drunk went on one of his binges. So, I didn't spend a whole lot of time in that apartment.

Most of my free time was spent hanging out at the student lounge at Judson, visiting friends and dodging the faculty, some of whom I'd made enemies with. One Sunday afternoon, Kathy and some friends and I were eating lunch in the cafeteria when a phone call came for me in the student services office on the second floor.

"Hello," I gasped, out of breath from running up the stairs.

"Hello, Gary, it's Marlo, " she said, sounding like she'd been crying. *My God! That crazy woman from Mexico! I thought I'd heard the last of her!*

"Hi, it…it's been a while," I forced the words out, wondering how she got a hold of this number. "How are you doing?"

"Gary, my…my father passed away last week, and I just wanted to see you again. Do you think you could come up for a couple of days?" Her voice was wavering, then she broke into tears. That was a favorite ploy of hers which always seemed to work on me. When would she, and what would it take for her to release the hold she had on me?

"Look, just give me some directions and I'll be there as soon as I can." I said, trying to be compassionate. After Marlo gave me turn-by-turn instructions, I hung up the phone, asking myself the same questions over and over: Why did I say that to her? What did I just set myself up for?

Marlo gave me a landmark or two in the detailed instructions to her house. She lived in Birmingham, Michigan, a small, but affluent suburb of Detroit. It would be about a six-hour drive, provided the old Ford held up. The following morning, I turned in my apartment key, packed everything in the back of the car, and drove to the gas station to pick up my last paycheck. The boss was furious at such a short notice. I just told him it couldn't be helped, I had a personal emergency.

There was a hint of green grass emerging along the sides of the interstate. The sun was bright in the cloudless sky, and the Monday morning traffic was pleasantly limited. The growl of the engine bore a smooth path down the highway. An occasional glance in the rearview mirror revealed a telltale trail of blue smoke. That didn't look good.

I rolled into Birmingham about 4:30 that afternoon, finding Marlo's house with little difficulty. Her directions had been fairly accurate. The house was on a quiet, tree-lined street, much like the rest of the residential part of town I'd driven through.

Marlo's mother's house was a two-story brick home exuding the same prosperity as a lot of the other homes in the area did. A well-manicured lawn framed the house. Greek statues sprang up from meticulously designed flower gardens all around the house. A powder blue '65 Stingray was parked in the driveway next to the garage. Nice car, I thought. I parked the old Ford on the street so it wouldn't lower the property value of the house if I parked it in the driveway. I walked to the side door and rang the bell. There was no answer, so I walked slowly back to my car, still wondering why I made this trip. Secretly, I wished Marlo would give me a good reason to break the shackles of this unbelievable relationship once and for all. I needed closure. Behind the wheel of the Ford, I surrendered to exhaustion and dozed off, still wondering.

Almost an hour later, I heard a car pull into the drive. Opening my eyes, I noticed it was getting dark. I climbed out of the car and walked up the drive to meet Marlo, trying hard to hide the fact I really didn't want to be there. We exchanged a measured embrace, then went into the house to meet her mother, who had just arrived with Marlo. The rest of the evening was filled with talking about old times. Not a word was mentioned about the death of her father, with the exception of the comment I made to Marlo about how sorry I was for her loss. *Why? I didn't kill him!*

The next morning, after breakfast, Marlo drove the Stingray to work and left her car, a shiny maroon '68 Cougar, parked in its place She commented that she loved driving the 'Vette, which belonged to her brother-in-law. I imagined it was just another way of drawing attention to herself. She worked for an advertising firm that handled accounts for one of the auto makers Detroit. The 'Vette most likely gave that look of distinction to her at her job.

After everyone left for work that morning, I busied myself with a quick diagnostic check of the old Ford's woes. I took out my tool box and removed one of the valve covers from the ailing 292. My suspicions confirmed about the short remaining life of the engine, I found metal shavings and a small piece of piston ring in the pooled oil on top of the cylinder head. Nothing I could do here would fix it, so I replaced the valve cover, thinking how delicate a procedure it would be to nurse the tired old Ford back to Elgin, much less all the way to Iowa.

After putting my tools back in the trunk, I decided to wash the two cars; mine and the Cougar. Mine, I would have to be careful with. The dirt on the faded beige paint concealed a lot of rusted areas. When Marlo's Cougar was thoroughly cleaned and detailed, down to the wire wheels, I went into the house, finding a set of keys hanging in the kitchen that looked like they might fit her car. I moved the Cougar around in the driveway into the shade to finish toweling it off.

That afternoon, Marlo arrived home around 4:45, noticing her prized Cougar was sitting in a different spot in the driveway. She immediately landed all over me for driving her car without permission. After being harangued needlessly about stealing someone's car and driving outside the parameters of an insurance policy, it was finally my turn.

Without uttering a word, I left her standing in the drive, running her mouth with her hands on her hips, to retrieve my overnight bag from the house. When I returned, with an arrogant look on her face, she was about to say something to me when I held up my hand as if to stop her words.

"Thought I was doing you a favor by washing your car. All I did was move it around in the driveway, but I guess I was wrong!" Feeling myself losing control, I continued anyway.

"I've wanted to say this since Mexico, but never had the nerve to. I guess I was afraid of hurting your feelings. What you need is someone who will allow you to dominate them. I'm sorry, I just can't do it anymore. Goodbye, Marlo. Tell your mom thanks for everything."

Marlo stood in the driveway looking at me in disbelief. The slight evening breeze carried a cloud of blue smoke from the engine starting up directly at her, making her wince. She turned and stomped into the house without looking back. Neither did I as I pulled away from the curb, heading down the street to the interstate. It felt good to rid myself of this nemesis. Now, it was time to get on with my life.

The steady drone of the crippled engine and the faint knocking of the broken push rod drowned out my thoughts as I crossed the Indiana line. A very painful part of my life was beginning to subside. Why does emotional pain have to be a part of growing up? Out of every bad mistake comes a growing experience. And I will be a stronger person for it. However, there was still a stabilizing force missing from my life.

It was close to midnight when I pulled up to the tollbooth. Entering the Chicago Skyway in East Gary, I shifted gears once more, nursing the Ford back up to highway speed. Just then, the inevitable happened. The shotgun blast of the engine disintegrating left a trail of motor oil and coolant to the emergency parking lane along the deserted Skyway. With both hands still in a death grip on the steering wheel, I sat there in hopeless desperation, wondering how this would all pan out.

After what seemed like an eternity, I roused out of a shallow sleep when a Skyway maintenance truck pulled up behind me with its emergency light flashing. Noticing I'd blown my engine, he offered to take me to a gas station he believed would still be open at the next exit.

What we found was a closed gas station, but there were lights on in the adjacent garage. Inside there were two seedy-looking mechanics working on a '57 Ford stock car. A mixed aroma of grease, transmission fluid, and human sweat hung heavily in the air. The two men straightened up from the engine compartment of the race car and looked me over. The first guy, who must have been the boss, wore a tattered, sleeveless Harley Davidson T-shirt. His ample belly cascaded over the waistband of his blue jeans. His partner, a young-looking tough with shoulder length black hair tied in a ponytail and wearing a pair of greasy coveralls, leaned against the fender of the race car, taking a long pull from a can of Budweiser.

"Can I help ya?" Big Belly asked, grinning at Long Hair.

"Yeah, I, uh, blew my engine on the Skyway. It's parked just above the Clark Street exit. I was wondering if you'd tow it down for me and take a look at it."

"Won't be able to until morning," Big Belly replied. "Gonna cost ya fifteen bucks, though. What kinda car is it?"

"'57 Ford two door post, just like this one," I said hopefully, gesturing toward the race car. "Say, you wouldn't just want to buy it, would you?" I figured it wouldn't hurt to ask.

"Yeah, I'll give ya twelve bucks for it." With that, he and Long Hair broke into uproarious laughter, while I stood there looking at the floor.

"Mind if I use your phone?" I asked, trying like hell not to break down in front of these guys. As a last resort, I decided to call Dad.

"Pay phone's out front," Big Belly offered, nodding to the phone booth under the street light in front of the station.

The phone rang several times at my parent's house. Finally, someone picked it up.

"Hello." Dad sounded just like anyone would at two in the morning.

"Dad? Dad, it's Gary." My voice began to crack.

"Son, how are you? Is everything okay?" He asked with genuine concern.

"I'm okay," I replied, but emotionally, I was on my knees. "Dad, I… uh…threw a rod in the Ford in Chicago tonight. I don't know what else to do. I'm broke and I just want to come home." Tears began to cloud my vision.

"Listen, Gary, just tell me where you are exactly, and we'll come and get you, okay?" Feeling a great weight being lifted from my shoulders, I gave Dad directions to the disabled Ford.

"Dad?"

"Yeah?"

"Thanks."

"See you when we get there. You be careful, okay?

"I will. 'Bye." I stood in the phone booth and stared at the cradled phone, then walked back into the garage.

"Thanks for all the help guys, " I half-heartedly volunteered. Big Belly and Long Hair acknowledged me with a wave as I motioned to the Skyway maintenance man that it was time to get out of there.

I explained to the maintenance man, finally identifying himself as just Chuck, what my plans were on the way back up to my car. I thanked Chuck for all his help as he placed a couple of road flares out to warn other traffic.

"You'll be okay to stay in your car, just lock it up," he cautioned.

Dad wasted little time getting to Chicago. About 8:15, I saw the familiar black Ford Galaxy slowing down on the opposite side of the Skyway. Turning around on the far side of the toll booth, he rolled to a stop behind me. Gayle had come with him. It was good to see them both, especially now. Dad's plan was to haul the old girl back home and see about getting her fixed, so they had gotten a neighbor out of bed to borrow his tow bar. I doubted fixing it was possible, but he always held out hope for hopeless situations.

The trip back to Iowa was a long one, but enjoyable. The three of us talked a lot about home, high school, college, and the war. It was slow going, though, with my car being towed behind us. We all took turns driving, because we all shared the same sleepless night.

Finally home, Dad and I unhooked the old Ford in the backyard under a big maple tree, where it would set for a few weeks. Another chapter in my life had come to a close. Part of the stabilizing force in that chapter was my dad.

Dad didn't have to drive to Chicago in the middle of the night to rescue me, but he did. That's what dads do. He never questioned me about my decisions, allowing me to make my own mistakes and learn from them. A man of few words, his cautionary advice whenever I went into Marshalltown at night, "no liquor", spoke volumes. Not that I always obeyed that directive, but just his saying that always told me to make good choices and be careful in the process.

Dad always taught my brother and I to be respectful to our elders, to ask favors as a last resort in troubled times, and to work hard toward any achievements in life. I revered his experiences in World War II asking him at times to expound on how he came across the German dagger he kept hidden away in a cupboard in the kitchen.

"Took it off a dead Nazi," he'd boldly tell me when I was much younger. "Traded it for a Hershey bar with a French farmer," he'd admit when I was in high school.

Dad would seldom speak of his experiences during the Battle of the Bulge. I always knew from those reactions, that he carried unwanted demons. Painful memories of fiery explosions and agonized screams of fallen comrades all needed to be buried and forgotten.

We had our differences over the years, Dad and I. He was always in charge, though. Subliminally teaching me to make decisions on my own, showing me simple carpentry skills, and teaching me how to drive a car, all served to prepare me for adulthood. Yes, Dad was a stabilizing force in my life. His influence would pave the way for my next step toward maturity.

8. Summer of '70: The Call

Throughout the spring and early summer of 1970, I had enjoyed a life unencumbered by tiresome academia. Another freedom I treasured was living at home, paying rent as if I were a boarder, and working to save a little money. The only thing my folks asked in return was the courtesy of informing them of my whereabouts. In a world of unfairness, that seemed more than reasonable. I found employment at a livestock feeder equipment factory in a small farming community about fifteen miles north of Albion, off Highway 14. Conrad, world-renowned as the 'Black Dirt Capitol,' was a typical small town where old friends meet at either the bank, post office, fire station, coffee shop, or grocery store that made up this heartland community, attempting to solve the problems of the world.

The vast majority of the townspeople worked at the plant. Some of them were Vietnam veterans. In my job, which varied from manning the small parts solvent booth, where barrels of steel plates multiplied faster than I could dip them insolvent in preparation for the paint booth; to the assembly line, then ultimately working as a spot welder, I came in daily contact with some of these vets. Some would relate to me incomparable tales of combat and the tragedy of a lost buddy, while others declared a ho-hum existence of drinking beer or pulling guard duty near Saigon for a year.

Over the next few months, I had become friends with and had grown envious of these combat seasoned veterans. Struggling to give their lives new meaning while trying to put their pasts behind them, these guys held the respect and admiration of their fellow heartlanders, as well as my own, It was just a matter of time until I would become a part of all this; the right of every American to answer the call of duty.

Nightly newscasts continued to chronicle the war. David Brinkley delivered commentaries on the U.S. bombings of North Vietnamese provinces and cities. The United States and its allies were determined to stop the spread of communism in this obscure third world country. Anti-war demonstrations on the home front also dominated the news. *Give peace a chance* was the battle cry of those who didn't understand the reasons behind this conflict. To them, any war was wrong.

Mid-May of 1970 marked the turning point of my young life. I contacted an army recruiter in Marshalltown to learn what my options were for enlisting. May's Iowa lottery number for the draft was 95, and my assigned number was 295. No chance of being drafted, but just in case, I wanted the choice to be mine.

Signing contracts allowing me to enter the inactive reserves, the recruiter would later give me an entry date for active duty. There was also a matter of completing a background investigation, and then finalizing the enlistment paperwork. He would bring everything to my home in a few days. I'd talked it over with my folks, and reluctantly they voiced their approval. Joining the army during these troubled times was not a path they would have me take, however.

The evening of May 19th marked the end of another warm Iowa spring day. The waning sun painted a golden glow on the farmland on the eastern edge of the small town. Cicadas in the trees were chirping their evening song. Mom was washing up the supper dishes when the olive drab Plymouth sedan with U.S Government markings on the doors pulled up in front of the house. In a small town like Albion, when neighbors saw an army sedan stop in front of a house, it meant one of two things: either an army chaplain and a casualty officer are calling on a family to inform them their son has been killed in combat, or a recruiter is putting in some long hours.

Sergeant First Class Robert Schiller climbed out of the sedan and strode briskly up the walk toward the house. A short, muscular man in his mid-thirties, he sported a small eagle tattoo on each forearm. His well-tailored, starched khakis displayed several rows of medals above his left breast pocket. The remaining sunlight glinted brightly off his highly polished brass.

Dad and I came out to meet Sergeant Schiller. As I expected, he found that common ground right away, launching into a long-winded recollection of a wartime experience. Chuckling and nodding his approval, Sergeant Schiller was probably thinking to himself, how many proud fathers have told me a similar story? I know I'd heard that one several times myself. Dad was telling the story about the time he was on guard duty at Fort Hood, Texas, and shot a major in the butt after he failed to identify himself. We all had a good laugh about the poor schmuck running through the woods screaming in pain, then went into the house to finish signing the enlistment papers.

After signing all the required papers, Sgt Schiller gave me the date I would enter active duty. I had until October 4th to tie up any loose ends. On that day, I would depart for basic training at a location to be determined at the entrance station in Des Moines. Then, on to Fort Monmouth, New Jersey for Advanced Individual Training in Automatic Data Processing Repair.

I was excited about the evening's outcome, but at the same time , my thoughts were filled with anticipation of the morning of October 4th. The words of the guys at the plant echoed in my mind: *Yeah, Uncle Sugar'll put you where he wants you.* My optimism always overshadowed their opinions, though.

Several weeks later, in a conversation with my older sister Bette, a nurse at Marshalltown Area Community Hospital, I discovered that an old friend, Marie Davis, worked with her as a nurse's aid . Marie and I hadn't seen or heard from each other for some time. The irony was, Marie wasn't aware that I was Bette's brother until she was showing wedding pictures of my brother Dennis and his new wife, Cathy, at work one day. I appeared in some of the pictures, striking a chord with Marie.

Bette called me, telling me about the revelation, and I called Marie for a date. I picked her up one night after her shift at the hospital. We continued dating, developing the close relationship we'd both searched for aimlessly for most of our young adult lives. The openness we shared put each of us totally at ease with the other.

That candor we shared, however, was not without hardship. Reluctantly, I told Marie I had enlisted in the army, and would leave for basic training the first week of October. She accepted it, though reasonably upset at the prospect of having a real relationship interrupted. My mother, being from the old school of thought where good girls don't call boys, particularly disliked the fact that Marie would call me at home, or would occasionally come over.

I seem to recall one lost afternoon; Marie and I had a date planned. It was the annual Labor Day celebration in Albion, and I'd planned to pick Marie up late in the afternoon for a teen club dance that evening, Well, I drank a little too much beer with friends and slept straight through the agreed rendezvous time. Marie phoned my house several times only to have Mom tell her I was asleep, and I would return her call when I woke up. Somehow, I never got the message that Marie had called repeatedly, and I encountered a great deal of difficulty and embarrassment explaining that to Marie. She thought it was funny that I got trashed and didn't call her back, but Mom, she wasn't that understanding.

"You should be thoroughly ashamed of yourself," she admonished.

A few days before I was to report to the draft board for the bus trip to Des Moines, I asked Marie to marry me. Our whirlwind courtship was remarkably short, but we both were certain that's what we wanted. We planned to be married that following August.

That night, some vet friends of mine from the factory threw a farewell keg party for me at Upper Pine Lake, near Eldora. One of the guys, a former Navy radioman, owned a small farm next to the lake. Hours had passed, and after having our fill of cold beer and burnt hotdogs, we all gathered around the bonfire to silently watch the glowing embers.

There was a noticeable sadness in that small gathering. These were very uncertain times. The guys sitting around the fire who had been off to war didn't understand why I enlisted, but they accepted me into the brotherhood of military service. The future didn't look too bright for our generation. We had to live for the day and grab happiness where we could. A lot of people our age were getting married just before young husbands were drafted, or shipped off to join the service. Vietnam meant certain death to those who went. Nobody thought of guys coming back. While the news often portrayed soldiers dying in battle, those who lived to return home were rarely mentioned. When I proposed to Marie, I gave no guarantees I wouldn't be sent to Vietnam. But, if I had to go, I would. It would be my duty.

Life was so simple before all this came about. The war. The sexual revolution. Following parental guidance. All this, together with searching for one's identity, brought forth a totally new set of confusing life rules. Our generation was given to the ideals that if you were going to die, why not live a little first?

Tearful farewells were exchanged that night at the lake. My brother Dennis vocalized his wishes that I didn't go. "There are always alternatives," he pleaded. "It's so stupid." It probably was stupid, but it was still my own decision, and I would see it through.

In the wee hours of the morning, most of the well-wishers had faded off into the darkness toward parked cars, then home. The time had come to say last goodbyes. Solemnly, my brother and I embraced, then shook hands without further words. Yes, these were uncertain times.

October 4th dawned with a cool, crisp freshness typical of Midwestern autumns. Driving into Marshalltown to the bus stop at the Selective Service office, we crossed the bridge over the Iowa River near Timmons Grove State Park. The remnants of autumn colors in the trees were beginning to dwindle. A light frost covered the recently-harvested corn fields near the river. Wispy columns of mist hung above the placid waters of the Iowa, giving the look of diamond-studded lace in the early morning light.

Taking in these wonders of nature, the realization hit me that little time would be afforded to enjoy my natural surroundings where I was headed. But, if the occasion did arise, would the perception be the same? The tension and rigors of boot camp would certainly limit my abilities to enjoy the beauty of nature.

A chartered bus was being loaded with baggage as we arrived at the draft board. Moms, dads, friends and loved ones were saying their last goodbyes to their patriot sons. Looking around at these guys, I could see the same fear I had, written on their faces. Fear of the unknown. Of course, there would be the arrogant ones who would be the self-proclaimed immortals. Those were the dangerous ones. The ones to stay clear of. Passing my suitcase off to the bus driver, I hugged Mom and Dad, with promises to write.

The reception station at Fort Des Moines was established within the walls of old Camp Dodge, dating back to World War I, near the airport. Very similar to college registration at MCC and Judson, any and all doubt about who you were and what your next move would be, was eliminated. Everything was done by precise movement, and by the numbers.

"Take this form, fill out the top three lines, then sign it in the bottom left-hand corner. Last name first, first name last, middle initial." Any poor disoriented souls were promptly placed on the right track.

"I said move up to the yellow line, recruit, now move your ass!"

The proverbial 'pink line' was real. Dozens of underwear-clad future heroes filed from one station to the next, answering questions, being poked and prodded, bled and peed.

"Awright, gimme two ranks right here, girls!" bawled a stocky sergeant in starched khakis. "Drop yer drawers to your knees and wait for the doctor. Do exactly what he says, and you'll get outa here faster!"

The final checkpoint was the transportation desk. That's where they told us where we'd be headed for basic training. Thinking I would draw Fort Leonard Wood, Missouri, just a mere two hundred miles from home,

I ended up assigned to Fort Lewis, Washington. Oh well, I conceded, I always wanted to visit the Pacific Northwest.

The U.S. Army flew me and seven other young, bright-eyed recruits to Omaha on a chartered King Air, where we boarded a United 727 for the final leg of the flight to Seattle-Tacoma. The flight was relaxing and enjoyable, except for several manly gestures made by the FT. Lewis-bound recruits who were refused to be served in-flight drinks by the flight attendants.

The first impression of a place is a lasting one. Touching down at Sea-Tac at six-thirty that evening, we were greeted by cold, rainy darkness. I would always think of that place as the most dismal place on earth.

After being loaded onto a bus and driven to the replacement center at North Ft Lewis, we learned very quickly how to stand at attention , march in single file, and be cold and wet to the bone without a whimper of complaint.

Every mother's son was thrust headlong into a man's world that night. Fears and apprehensions about a strange, new environment, were compounded by darkness and rain. Our group of cherub-faced recruits, or fish, they called us, was greeted by a rank of mean-looking Drill Sergeants leering at us from beneath the brims of their *Smokey the Bear hats.* These guys really had mean and ugly down to a science.

Everyone was issued an old field jacket and two blankets, then marched to some old WWII era transient barracks. Along the way, we marched past a small group of 'old timers', Privates, PFC's, and Corporals, standing under a street light, showering us with cat-calls and jeers meant to either rattle us or welcome us to the army.

"Hey look, new meat!"

"Left right, left right, left,left,left. Haw haw haw!"

"Hey, whaddya lookin' at? Look straight ahead, 'cruit!"

"Awright you guys, knock it off," defended our DI. Hey, this guy's okay, I thought to myself. Maybe this won't be so bad after all.

The following morning was clear and cool. Puddles of water in the gravel streets still marked the passing of last night's rain. The warming sun helped give a new outlook on things. I took a good look at the area we arrived at last night. The reception center down the street was a huge auditorium, more imposing from the outside, emerging from a grove of pine trees along the gravel streets.

While in the latrine shaving, I looked in the mirror at my mutton-chop sideburns and long hair for the last time. With a grimace, I shaved off the sideburns into an envelope to send home to Marie. The hair, well, that would be taken care of later.

The DI that marched and defended us last night from the prior-service wolf pack, entered the barracks at 0630, making sure we were all up and ready for the day. Everyone was ready to go. Heaven help anyone who overslept on this, a day of new beginnings.

Following an Army breakfast of eggs, bacon, grits and a wide assortment of fresh fruit, the day progressed though a series of briefings, more by-the-number instructions, and *smoke-'em-if-ya-got-'em* breaks.

The following morning, the DI's marched us to the barber shop. The part dreaded by most of us was close at hand. Carefully coiffed, long-treasured locks fell to the floor at the feet of the masochistic barbers. These guys were very detached and objective about their work. Barber shop conversation? Forget it. Some of the recruits joked with their barbers about trimming around the edges and a little off the top. Once in a while, a barber would crack a smile, but mostly, the comments were ignored. Periodically, a recruit would tear up, watching his long tresses hit the floor.

The freshly-shorn platoon of recruits was then marched to a huge warehouse filled with rows of long tables piled high with government-issued clothing and equipment. Wire bins of helmets, boots and field gear sat behind the tables. In alphabetical order, we filed slowly down the line giving sizes of underwear, pants, shirts, boots, and hats until each of us were lugging two duffel bags of o.d. green government issue.

The next two weeks were filled with instructions on how to wear the uniform and polish boots, classes on military customs and courtesies, and how to recognize each rank from Private to General. During that time, we were also introduced to the dreaded air gun. To speed up mass inoculations, the Army began using a compressed air gun, a veritable skin ripper if muscles were flinched or flexed at the wrong time.

The next nine weeks was a journey through a world of madness, spirit-breaking training, ruthless Drill Instructors, exhausting days and sleepless nights. Throughout our training days outside, C141 Starlifters and C5 Galaxies screamed overhead, departing adjacent McCord Air Force Base to the west. These guys are headed for Vietnam, we imagined. Once in a while, a watchful DI would chastise us for watching the planes taking off.

"Take a good look, girls!" he'd yell. "Someday, you'll be on one of those! If you keep lookin' up, you'll get on one, go to 'Nam and never come back, 'cause you ain't payin' attention to your Drill Instructor! Now get down and start doin' push-ups 'til I start sweatin'!"

I must have averaged three hundred a day. Sure paid off, though. Fear of extra push-ups and rabid DI's was instilled in us all, but sideways glances at the huge planes roaring overhead continued to be discreetly stolen.

Just before Thanksgiving, I called Marie from a payphone outside the mess hall. Before I left for boot camp, I'd asked her to marry me. I had loved her since the night I met her at the coffee house, and knew somehow we would spend the rest of our lives together. Given all the circumstances, I wasn't quite sure I wanted to wait until August. The more we talked that day, the more set we both were on moving up the wedding date. We would be married before Christmas, come hell or high water.

The funny thing about changing our original wedding plans was that Marie has always been outspoken, unafraid to speak her mind. That was one of the things I loved her for. She obtained a blood test back in Marshalltown, and permission from my folks, because I was underage. I had just turned twenty in October. Mom refused to sign the forms so we could be married, so Marie took the matter in hand.

"That's fine," she replied to the roadblock Mom threw up. "Missouri's not that far away, and we'll get married with or without your presence or consent." Missouri's age of consent was only eighteen. Mom relented, accepted Marie's wishes, and signed the waiver.

All the rifle ranges, confidence courses, PT tests, and written exams were behind us now, and the final exam was just days away. The final test would determine who would earn their 'mosquito wings' Private stripes earned upon graduation from basic training.

The big day finally came. I was one of thirty-five or so out of our company that earned that first stripe. We had our new stripes quickly sewn on and stood proudly in the auditorium listening to speeches congratulations, and cautions about the days and months to come.

"Rely on your training," boomed a Sergeant Major, the keynote speaker from the Training Brigade.

That day, I'd felt so much pride in what I'd accomplished, where I was at, and where I was going. One thing had changed, though. I no longer fantasized about being a super hero. I was merely a patriot. A patriot son.

At the conclusion of the graduation ceremony, the DI's marched our company back to the barracks to pick up our duffle bags and order packets. Ours jobs here were done. My orders read, Company B, 113th Student Signal Battalion, Ft Monmouth, New Jersey. For the draftees, however, the orders reading places like, Infantry Training Brigade, Ft Lewis, Washington, and various army posts around the country, was not such good news.

Members of 1st Platoon, E Co, 1ˢᵗ BN, 2ⁿᵈ Student BDE bid each other goodbye and good luck, with promises to keep in touch. Emotions ran mixed; some guys were headed to Ft. Monmouth, some to FT Belvoir, Virginia for mechanic's school, others to infantry training. To this day, I've never crossed paths with anyone I shared the pain and frustration of basic training with. We were all patriot sons with a different job to do.

9. A New Frontier

The dayroom of the white-washed WWII-style barracks was lined with duffle bags of the new arrivals. Young fresh-faced privates swapped war stories about boot camp and the glory days to come.

"At ease!" someone yelled, bringing a hush over the crowded room. A short, stocky sergeant walked in, quickly measuring each of us with a practiced eye. He wore starched fatigues and a blue helmet liner identifying him as Signal School cadre.

"Gentleman, I'd like to welcome you to the Signal Center and School," he said in a thick Latino accent. "My name is Master Sergeant Villareal. I am the non-commissioned officer in charge of the in-processing center. When you've completed your in processing, you'll be assigned to a student company. If your classes don't begin right away, your asses will belong to your First Sergeant. Any questions? Good. Now fall outside with your gear and get on the buses. Move it, people!" Wow! That guy didn't play around! He must have been around for a hundred years and made that speech every day of his life.

The fact that our asses belonged to the First Sergeant couldn't have been plainer. Six of us were going to the ADP Repair course, which didn't begin until the first week of January. Being part of the elite group called the 'zero weekers', we all drew KP duty.

Zero week was a lot like hell week at college. Brand new privates fresh from basic training received a further, somewhat harsh introduction to Army life. We had zero identity and zero responsibility, except to do exactly as we were told, without question.

Kitchen police had its drawbacks. The hours were exhaustingly long-- up every morning at 0400 to set up serving lines, fill milk dispensers, and perform various odd jobs at the beckon call of some overweight sergeant, until after eight o'clock every night.

During the daylight hours, if we did a good job for this portly cook, we were rewarded with a little time off to take care of personal business, plus enjoy all the food we could eat. When the head cook released us after a long day, the first stop would be the bowling alley for a cold beer. Strains of Led Zeppelin and Creedence Clearwater Revival blared from the jukebox, blocking out the thoughts of the day.

After about ten days of KP, I'd just about had enough. I performed every job in the mess hall from DRO (dining room orderly), scrubbed an endless lineup of pots and pans, and cleaned the outside grease trap. Looking more and more like a dead end for me, they could take this whole building and stuff it where the sun doesn't shine! Balling my fists, gritting my teeth, and cussing to myself, I vented my frustrations.

The mess sergeant must have been watching me from the loading dock door. Seeing my behavior as a plea for some fatherly advice, he walked over to where I was sitting by the open grease trap. Even as I stood up, the massive Black sergeant towered head and shoulders over me.

"Son," he offered in a deep, gentle voice, "whatever happens in this life or this mans' army, never loose your sense of humor." With that, he turned and walked back into the mess hall.

Those profound words would never be forgotten, nor will the sound of the kind, old sergeant's voice. Still today, I pass the them along to those who look like they need a lift, or just a shot of my brand of humor.

On the afternoon of 15 December, the Signal School began closing down for Christmas break, and classes would be suspended until 2 January. Since most of the men on the company had flight reservations for that afternoon. The First Sergeant lined everyone up in the dayroom for a uniform and haircut check. A makeshift barbershop was set up in the corner of the room to give any needed trims at a dollar each.

Travel money always seemed to be problem for some, so the company commander had a pay table in his office. Unaware of the hidden consequences of taking what was called *casual pay*, I signed up for what I thought was a Christmas bonus. The extra cash would come in handy, I reflected, 'cause I'll be a married man in a few days.

My bride-to-be met me at the passenger terminal at the Waterloo Airport late that wintry afternoon. Winding my way through the crowd arriving passengers, I caught a glimpse of Marie excitedly waving outside the gate. Making my way over to her, we stood embracing amid the crush of the holiday travelers. Holding her after fourteen weeks was well worth the long wait. I felt safe in her arms.

"I missed you so much," she whispered in my ear. "Everything's all set. Sunday at one-thirty, we'll be married. Aren't you excited?"

"Yes, in more ways than one," I replied with a wink, pulling her close for one more deep kiss.

Marie sat very close to me as we drove south out of Waterloo. Our thoughts were on Sunday afternoon, as snow flurries began to dance in the beam of the headlights. Not enough to make the roads slick yet, the light snow served as a reminder of how unpredictable an Iowa winter can be.

The Jackson Five's *I'll Be There* played on the car radio as the snow began to fall heavier. The translucent blanket seemed to part to either side, allowing the car to glide through the winter night. Everything was right. Marie and I were one. I held her tightly as we turned off the main highway and headed for my folks' place in Albion.

After spending the evening with my folks reminiscing and swapping war stories with Dad, I drove Marie home. Along the way, we talked and laughed together like young lovers, debating on names for our first born. Both wanting a boy, we would call him Chad Michael. Through sickness and health, richer and poorer times, we would grow together.

Sunday morning had finally arrived. Dad had been up for hours, and was sitting in the living room reading the Sunday paper. Mom was puttering in the kitchen baking cookies and putting together trays of mints for the wedding reception.

"Good morning, sleepyhead," she greeted as I walked into the kitchen, "I thought you were going to sleep all day. It's getting late, and you have to be at the church in less than three hours."

"Good morning to you too, Mom," I replied with a sideways glance. Mom overdid things a bit sometimes, but she always meant well. Before I even was out of bed, she had pressed my uniform so I could take care of other details. Getting married was a big step in my life. I was pretty nervous, but Mom kept calming me down. Her job was not yet finished.

The small chapel in the First Methodist Church in Marshalltown held an intimate gathering of the closest friends and relatives from both of our families. The pianist played a medley of Simon and Garfunkel tunes along with our favorite, *I'll Be There.*

It was a happy time of the year. The spirit of Christmas made our wedding day even more special to Marie and I. After years of on and off togetherness, and a short few weeks of dating, we would be united in marriage. Beginning a new life together was intriguing and romantic. We were on our way, and nothing could stop us.

My nervousness began to increase as I watched with great anticipation, Marie being escorted down the isle toward the altar by her father. She was a beautiful bride in her street length dress of white velvet and lace, carrying a red rose and daisy pompom. She was wearing that same confident, warm smile she was the night I met her. As we turned to face the minister, my mind was racing with thoughts of missing a cue and screwing up my vows, and when the minister recites the part about speaking now or holding your peace, somebody would jump up and yell, "Wait a minute, hold everything!"

Marie did have to give me a discreet poke in the ribs when I absentmindedly failed to repeat my vows in a timely fashion, drawing a chuckle from the minister, Dennis, my brother and best man; and Marie's sister Karen, her maid of honor. I didn't want to look at faces of family and relatives to see who else had noticed my little brain lock.

After the ceremony, Dave Hansen took the standard array of happy couple, group, and family photos. He had amiably agreed to photograph our wedding. Funny thing about Dave doing this for us, was that for the past three years, I honestly thought Marie was his girlfriend. Even though nobody mentioned their relationship, I never aggressively pursued a relationship with her until I enlisted. It was only after Marie and I discovered the chemistry between us during the summer, did I realize she and Dave were nothing more than close friends. Lessons learned sometimes can cause one to kick oneself in the butt.

Our appearance at our own wedding reception at Marie's folk's home in Melbourne was a cursory one. Cutting the wedding cake and unwrapping gifts are very small, but integral parts of the wedding tradition which allow certain rascals adequate time to screw with the getaway car, another important part of that special event.

Leaving the reception after about an hour and a half, Marie and I viewed with a mixture of horror and resigned acceptance, her new red Maverick covered with shaving cream, old shoes and tin cans tied to the rear bumper, and crumpled newspapers filling the interior from floor to ceiling. Not bad enough, not until we'd removed all the newspapers did we noticed the additional trap awaiting us. The perpetrators had covered the front seat with a slimy layer of shaving cream as well!

The next five days were spent getting to know each other physically and spiritually. We emerged from hiding at Marie's apartment in Waterloo only three times those few days: once to buy a small Christmas tree from a lot in town, then to spend Christmas eve with our folks, and finally for a late night pizza. Marital bliss added a rosy glow to our cheeks and happiness in our hearts for each other.

New Years Day brought severe winter storm warnings for most of the state of Iowa. Heavy snow, gale-force winds and sub-zero temperatures were expected. Because I had to report back to Ft. Monmouth no later than the 5th of January, a good idea would be to head back a few days early to beat the storm. Marie had planned to stay behind, finishing out the winter semester at the University of Northern Iowa.

Early the next morning, after a lingering and tearful farewell, I left Melbourne, heading east for New Jersey. Already starting to snow appreciably, it was a prelude to one of the worst January blizzards in recent Iowa history. Central Iowa was covered in more than three feet of snow, with high winds building up car-covering and door-blocking drifts. Marie and her folks were snowed in for more than two days. Melbourne and Marshalltown were virtually shut down. State Highway 30 was closed from Marshalltown to Des Moines, a distance of about sixty miles.

Beating the storm back to New Jersey, I had rented a tiny forty-by-eight trailer house outside of Farmingdale, a tiny bedroom community about twelve miles from Ft. Monmouth. By the end of January, Marie had completed her classes at UNI in Cedar Falls, and we were united once more. Our first home wasn't much, but it was cozy and affordable, and we were together.

After rent and other expenses, our spending was severely limited. Having learned that the 'Christmas bonus' was no more than an advance on the next month's pay, things began to look mighty bleak for us. As a matter of survival, we resorted to ingenious ways of cutting corners. We ate a lot of macaroni, washed clothes in the bathtub by hand, and searched for spare change for gas and cigarettes under the car seats and couch cushions. For entertainment, we flew homemade kites on the deserted beach at Asbury Park.

Friends at the Signal School liberated salt and pepper shakers, individual boxes of cereal, sugar, and some fruit from the mess hall for us. A milk machine across the drive from our house in the trailer park was vandalized several times, leaving the coin box empty and the front door open. Financially strapped GI's living in the trailer park often took advantage of that inviting opportunity, stopping and grabbing several half gallons of the beneficial white liquid on their way to work. Keeping ourselves in free milk for several weeks without remorse, the owners of the doomed machine got tired of fixing it almost daily, and removed it from the premises.

The antequainted oil furnace in our tiny home never seemed to put out enough heat to keep us warm. During the coldest months of the winter, it quit working altogether. We'd wake up to surprises of seeing our breath and ice in the toilet. Jumping out of bed and quickly dressing, I would throw Marie's clothes under the blanket to warm them up, then run out the door to start the car so we could be in a warm place.

Finally, one frigid evening while I was on the four to eleven shift at the ADP class, Marie had had enough of the faulty furnace, the maintenance man never really being able to keep it running for more than two days, and the icy conditions in the house. Storming up to the manager's house, she kicked open the door to his double-wide, stood in the doorway, towering over the terrified man and his wide-eyed wife who had just sat down to a sumptuous dinner.

"You can take yourself and your wife down to *my* house and freeze *your* asses off for a while!" she snarled, with fire in her eyes. That guy just made the wrong lady mad at him.

"I'm staying right here until that damned furnace is fixed and fixed right this time!"

Needless to say, the furnace was fixed that very night. At least we thought it was. It would come on, heating the house for several days. Then, without warning, it would fail to come on in the middle of the night. We just adapted to the inconvenience, hoping for spring to arrive and give us some relief from the cold and that stupid furnace.

Slowly, things in the ADP school were going south for me. With basic electronics successfully behind me, the binary language of computer logics left me hopelessly confused. The harder I tried, the less sense it was all making.

Changing to a different career field seemed like a viable option to total failure, so with the understanding help of the School Brigade Chaplain and my company commander, I was transferred to a still photography course beginning in just a few days.

While waiting for the new course to begin, I was given a little extra time to take care of personal business. The weather had started to warm up a bit, and new leaves were beginning to bud in the trees. One afternoon, I was at home thinking how gratifying it was to see wintry weather finally give way to warm spring sunshine. Standing in the small living room, I stared at the thermostat, wondering. I grabbed a screwdriver from the drawer in the kitchen, removed the cover, and to my amazement, a broken wire inside appeared to be the root of all the problems. With a little solder and tightening a few screws, the old furnace was humming like a top. But it was almost eighty degrees outside. I sure wished I'd thought of that when we were freezing to death in that place.

After the transfer to the photo course, things looked much brighter for Marie and me and my military career. Thoroughly enjoying the transition to a career path I understood, tangible rewards would be reaped for years to come. I gained a deep satisfaction from what I liked to call 'creating pictures' with a camera.

In June of 1971, I graduated not with honors, but with dignity, from Still Photography Course 71-02. Of a class of National Guardsmen, two other regular Army soldiers and I received reassignment orders to our first permanent party stations. Secretly, I'd hoped for Vietnam, but with the change to the new school, chances of going were slim to none. The Air Force and civilian media had taken over the role of combat photography.

Brooke Army Medical Center at Ft. Sam Houston in San Antonio was my first assignment as an Army photographer. Ironically, out of the class of fifteen future Army photographers at Ft Monmouth, I was the lone recipient of an assignment as a medical photographer. Gross amputations, severe burn injuries, and mutilations from explosions were depicted in graphic detail during the classroom training, and having never been exposed to such horrendous and disfiguring injuries, I distinguished myself by losing my lunch during a block of instruction on medical photography.

Marie and I were excited about the assignment to Ft. Sam. San Antonio was a romantic city, filled with history and beauty, However, one more hurdle we'd have to overcome in our growing marriage was another separation. I would have to leave for San Antonio alone, and she would have to fly down to join me at our new post later. Driving away from Marie's parents house toward Highway 30 and southbound to Texas, I watched her in my rear view waving goodbye with tears in her eyes.

The lonely road trip to San Antonio was like retracing my steps on the trip to Mexico two years earlier. The same route, the same truck stops and restaurants greeted me with familiarity.

San Antonio was all that I had imagined. Marie and I had gotten into the custom of doing library research on new places we would be sent to, and what we could see and do, and our new home had a lot to offer. The old city was nestled in the rolling hills and river valley around the Alamo, Texas's center of history.

Brooke Army Medical Center was a sprawling army post on the north edge of the city. From a distance, its unmistakable white wooden barracks and orange and white checkered water tower marked it as a military installation. Lining the vast parade quadrangle were red tile-roofed buildings painted a pale yellow. The main hospital, a grand old three story brick building, sat at one end of the parade field, guarded by the post flag pole. Toward the opposite end of the massive parade field, along the main drag through post, was the Department of Pathology building, my new place of duty.

My responsibility as a photographer in the pathology department was to assist the many different departments at Brooke with pictorial support, ranging from autopsies, to gross specimens of organs, to detailing the reconstructive surgical progress of severe burns, as well as a plethora of other injuries. Brooke was a reconstructive center for casualties of the Vietnam War, and enjoyed a world-renowned reputation for successful treatment of injured war veterans.

One of the most gut-wrenching experiences for me, was photographing in the morgue next door, the body of a sixteen year old son of a career officer. The troubled youth had tragically taken his own life with a twelve gauge shotgun, nearly decapitating him. Scenes of medical photography training flashed through my mind as nauseating repulsion gave way to an objective fascination as I stared at the young boy's gaping wounds. At some point, I replaced the thought of that kid ever being a living, breathing human being with that of him being just another photographic subject.

Many other circumstances I had met with were both either unspeakably horrific or very fulfilling. Never knowing who , or what, would walk or be wheeled through the studio door, I developed a daily routine of glancing through the appointment book to gain as much information about the type of injury I would pictorialize, the age and sex of the patient, and any special needs they may have had.

One day, a helicopter pilot who had been shot down by enemy small arms fire near the Cambodian border, walked into the studio to have a series of healing-in-progress photos taken. His face, chest, and hands were severely burned, rendering him barely recognizable as a human being. CW2 William Stanfield was in his early thirties, and by Providence had survived the fiery crash of the OH-6 light observation helicopter only to endure years of pain and suffering through countless reconstructive surgeries. However, the physical pain he was subjected to held no comparison to the constant revulsion he faced at the hands of an ungrateful society.

Weeks of exposure to such human tragedies had highly educated me about objectivity, looking far beyond first impressions. The young pilot's face was hideously disfigured by the inferno of the crash, and gnarled stumps had replaced his fingers. His personality, however, seemed undaunted by his severe injuries. Humbled by his warm, cordial, educated demeanor, I shook his hand, offering him a seat.

Mr. Stanfield and I talked at length before I took the photos his plastic surgeon needed. I learned he was on the counseling staff at BAMC for combat injury related psychological problems most war-wounded veterans had to bear. CW2 Stanfield taught me a lot that day about relating to those soldiers who suffered debilitating battle injuries, whether that damage was physical, emotional, or both. Chief Stanfield had every reason to hate himself, his country and society for his catastrophic injuries. Some guys were like that, but not this man. He used his misfortune to help others heal their wounds.

Some guys wept openly about their injuries and battle experiences when they entered the studio for physician-ordered photos, while others would fly into a rage, raving about how the Army and society were trying to screw them over. One afternoon, a young SP4 whose face was shattered by a grenade, entered the studio, grabbed a huge amber ash tray off my desk and hurled it across the room. He reacted in the only manner he was capable of, I imagined, to my greeting of *'Hi, how's it going?'* Yet, still others responded in the same manner as CW2 Stanfield did--accepting their injuries while helping others deal with theirs.

By the end of the first week of September 1971, Marie had arrived in San Antonio. Together once again, we drove to the apartment I had rented in Alamo Heights, in the heart of a wooded historical area on a hill overlooking the city. The small apartment was in the back of a beautiful old house in a quiet neighborhood. The screen-in back porch was covered with honeysuckle vines which protected the back of the house from the blazing afternoon Texas sun.

Marie and I savored several more months in our comfortable little apartment. Growing ever closer together, we anticipated the celebration of our first wedding anniversary. Financially, we felt far more secure than we did in New Jersey. No longer did we search for hidden treasure under couch cushions and car seats.

Inevitably, the dark cloud of separation once more loomed on the horizon. After a few short months at Ft Sam Houston, I received orders for the Panama Canal Zone, with a reporting date of 25 January '72. Thinking it was absurd to receive relocation orders so soon, I accepted the transfer with an open mind. The appeal of going to Panama began grow, and we gathered all the information we could about the country, its culture, and the history of the canal from the post library and the Army Community Service office to start planning our next move.

Unfortunately, our careful planning had hit an unforeseen snag. Since I was a Spec 4 with less than three years in service, command sponsorship was not possible. To the Army, that meant if I'd met the prerequisites, I would be obligated for a three year tour in Panama, and Marie's air fare would be paid by Uncle Sam. What it meant to us, however, was that once again, I would have to go on ahead, finding a suitable place for us to live, then send for Marie, and the cost of the flight would be on us.

The morning of 23 January 1972, the temperature in San Antonio was a bone-chilling seventeen degrees. Dressed in winter greens, I boarded a TWA 727 at San Antonio International bound for Charleston Air Force Base to connect with a MAC flight to Howard Air Force Base in the canal Zone. As the plane raced along the runway and climbed into the chill morning air, I closed my eyes, thinking to myself, "Two weeks, Babe, I'll see you in two weeks."

10. Panama, Land of Contrast

The emerald waters of the Caribbean melded into the lush jungles of the Isthmus of Panama along the final approach course into Howard Air Force Base. As the 727 touched down, my mind was reeling with thoughts of enjoying life in this tropical paradise. *Crusoe and his girl Friday walking barefoot along white sandy beaches. Marie and Gary sipping pina coladas under the swaying palm trees.*

Like walking close to an open blast furnace, the tropical heat held me in its grip as I emerged from plane and walked across the tarmac to the passenger terminal. Wearing winter dress greens seemed like a good idea when I left San Antonio, but as the rivulets of sweat ran down my back, I grabbed the first chance that came along to change into lighter, more comfortable khakis,

Once the annoying, but always necessary processing-in ritual had been completed, my fellow 'newbies' and I were bused to our designated units. I would be assigned to the Strategic Communications Command South (STRATCOM) headquarters in Corozal. Down the road about three miles, creature comforts such as the mail room, mess hall, theatre, and PX, were located at Ft. Clayton. Along the highway to Clayton, a Bogardesque jungle landscape unfolded on either side of the road.

Part of the initiation rite of breaking fledgling photographers in at the photo lab in Corozal meant shooting officer and NCO dining-in parties two or three nights a week. Taking part in the traditional rituals of the *smoking lamp*, the antics of *Mr. Vice*, and following the strict orders of the president of the mess at these hail and farewell functions, all seemed sort of silly to me, but were vital steps in a military career, particularly in the officer ranks.

Trying not to be judgmental, I was there to photograph each event, however ordinary, unusual, or tasteless. I recall shooting a Colonels' tricycle race at one party. Late in the evening, after all the general officers retired for the evening, a makeshift race track was set up along the perimeter of the dining hall, and six bird colonels sat comically mounted on their miniature steeds, waiting for Mr. Vice to yell, 'Gentlemen, start pedaling!' Now, half of these guys were pretty well hammered at race time, which made this career builder more hilarious to watch.

Around the track they raced, running into tables, falling over like Arty Johnson on *Laugh-In*. Like a Roman chariot race, there was always a winner, always someone injured, but a good time had by all.

Mixing diplomacy and deceit became a fine art for me after shooting several of these evening events.

"Hey Specialist, take a snapshot of me with the General," an inebriated senior officer would demand. *I make pictures, you moron, I don't do snapshots.*

"Yes sir," I responded tactfully, "if you'll stand right over here by the flags. Hold it---that's good. One more, please---got it." Another satisfied customer.

Then there was the drunk who wouldn't remember I took his picture.

"Hey Shmitty, take my picture!"

"No problem, sir. Smile." (flash)

"Thanks! Gimme a couple eight by tens!"

"Sure thing, sir," I replied obediently. The trick was to leave the slide in the film back of the old Minolta 220 and just click the shutter, popping the flash at them. Most of those young officers were too drunk to know the difference, anyway.

With the predetermined reunion for Marie and I just a week away, I located a studio apartment in Panama City. On the sixth floor of a building along the busy El Central in the heart of the city, the two room apartment offered a partially obstructed view of the Bay of Panama, overlooking the rusted tin roofs of tenement buildings.

At two o'clock in the morning, two weeks to the day after I kissed her goodbye in San Antonio, I picked Marie up at Tocumen Airport on the outskirts of Panama City. All the horror stories I'd heard about being hassled by Panamanian customs officials diminished as a sleepy-eyed guard waved her through the gate, and into my arms.

Marie seemed content with our tiny corner of the world above the city, but with two exceptions. First of all, El Carnival, Panama's Mardi Gras, was in full swing. The constant drum beat and revelry in the street below lasting far into the night was more than anyone could take. Next, there was the elevator. The only alternative to walking up six flights of stairs doubled as a public restroom for kids and street people, always wreaking of stale urine.

One day, I arrived home from work to find Marie packing everything in large boxes. The panic I felt walking in on such a shocker quickly dissipated when I saw that familiar smile on her face.

"Honey," she said cheerfully, "you'll never guess what I did today."

"I give up. What?" I asked, still a little apprehensive.

"I found us a new apartment! A lady on the bus today was telling me she and her husband are leaving in a few days, and that we could rent their apartment if we'd want to. I told we'd take it. I just needed to get out of this place before I went bananas!" Marie rarely complained about anything, but when she did, there was good reason for it.

That next night, a friend from the lab helped us move all our belongings in the two large boxes to our new home, far from the constant din of the carnival. The quiet streets of Bella Vista, in an upper class section of the city near the American Embassy, were lined with large, Mediterranean-style homes.

Once again, we made a home in a small apartment in the back of a large house. We certainly had no complaints about this one. The homey flat would keep us comfortable for the next year or so. The terraced back yard would sustain us with a multitude of tropical fruit. Banana, coconut, lemon, and avocado trees and an assortment of fruit-bearing plants abounded.

Marie found a position teaching third grade students at a private Parochial school for embassy children in El Carmen, an upscale part of town near the University of Panama. Having no work permit, she and other American wives were paid $200 a month in cash, with a caution to tell any inquisitive immigration official that no money was accepted for their services; they were strictly volunteers.

Several months later, we moved to a larger apartment within walking distance of the school. Mike and Barb Perkins lived across the hall from our new home. Barb taught fifth grade at the school, while Mike was an intelligence analyst at Ft. Amador. In his job, he maintained dossiers on prominent political and military figures throughout Central and South America. The Perkins' were from Austin, Texas and spoke with the faint Texas twang of educated people. The four of us became friends, sharing common grounds that many military couples find in a foreign country: talking of places we'd been, places we'd go, traveling, going to the beach, shopping for artifacts, and barbequing.

A fifth grade student of Barb's, Mia Schumann, tutored Marie and I in conversational Spanish. Mia was very mature for her age, and a very efficient teacher. There was a great deal of hidden pain in her life, however. One evening, after our tutoring session, She revealed to us the torment her family endured.

Mia's father, Dr. Josef Schumann, was a Panamanian citizen of Swedish origin. Years earlier, he had brought his family to Panama, to experience the diverse culture and educational system. A literary critic and political activist, Dr. Schumann had written several articles for national newspapers such as La Prensa and Critica, proclaiming weaknesses in the education system and publicizing articles decrying rampant corruption in the government and the military structures of Panama.

Dr. Schumann was arrested and incarcerated as a political prisoner, being shuttled back and forth between the Guardia Nationale prison and Coiba Island, Panama's dreaded Devil's Island. Nearly beaten to death several times, authorities would transport him to Santa Rosa Hospital in Panama City for treatment, and always leave him unguarded. Afforded countless opportunities to escape, Dr. Schumann became increasingly suspicious, never taking the chance to free himself. Instead, he continued to write subversive articles on scraps of paper, gum wrappers, and even toilet paper. Within a year, he had written and smuggled to his family a twelve volume diary, each volume more incriminating to the Torrijos regime than the last.

Seemingly, the sole reason Schumann wasn't beaten to death was that newspapers in other Latin American nations were aware of his status as a political prisoner. Panamanian Secret Police officials wanted to make his possible death resemble a fatal illness, or being killed while trying to escape. They were cautious with the severe beatings.

One August evening, while I was away at the NCO Academy at Ft Sherman on the Atlantic side of the Isthmus, Marie gave in to her curiosity about the diary, picking up the phone to call Mia.

"Hi, Mia, it's Marie," she said, hearing a faint click in the line. "I was wondering if you could bring one of the diary volumes with you tonight."

"Uh...sure," Mia relied with hesitant apprehension. "I'll be over at seven."

Feeling troubled by her risky request, Marie stepped across the hall to speak to Mike. He would have the right answers, she thought.

"I just called Mia and asked her to bring one of the diaries over tonight," she admitted to Mike. "Should I have done that over the phone?"

"Oops," Mike replied, contemplating the consequence of the call. "Maybe not. Which one did you ask for?"

"None in particular---just one of them. Something else scares me, though," Marie replied with consternation in her voice. "I heard a click in the line while I was talking to Mia."

Mike gave her a wide-eyed look as if she had just done irrevocable harm to the Schumann family. "Uh, there's a chance her phone was tapped. Maybe yours, too. I noticed a click in my phone today."

"Call Mia back and ask her to bring the diary on Argentina," Mike suggested. "That should confuse the spooks."

Later that evening, Marie was reading the diary Mia had brought over earlier. It was the one on the political structure of the government and the military. In it, Omar Torrijos was implicated in a complex embezzling scheme, laundering millions through Swiss banks. Further, a young Lieutenant in the Torrijos regime, Manuel Noriega, was marked as the most likely successor to Torrijos. The General's demise was also outlined in great detail. A helicopter crash, engineered by a group of so-called loyalists, was to claim the life of the revolutionary hero.

Marie's ability to comprehend the dangerous contents of the diary, written entirely in Spanish, was limited at best. She had understood enough to become frightened of the consequences of its possession. To become entangled in a web of international intrigue was not her intention when she became interested in the contents of the diary. In a cold sweat, she got up to go across the hall. Mike would know how to handle this.

"Oh, you scared me!" she gasped as she reached for the doorknob to step into the hallway. Mike was standing at the door, ready to knock with a volume of the diary in his hand.

"We need to talk," he said, holding up his copy of the diary. Mia had dropped off a copy of the same one Marie had asked for earlier that evening.

"What are we going to do with this stuff, Mike?" Marie asked frantically, pulling him inside and closing the door.

"Right now, I have no idea, but if the same bozos that are tapping our phones are watching the building like I think they are, we're in some deep shit."

"I can't say exactly how I found this out," Mike continued, "but the good doctor was taken to Santa Rosa Hospital today. With all the beatings he's taken, he's got some inner ear damage and some internal bleeding."

"This whole thing gives me the creeps, " Marie shuddered. "What about his family?"

"I'll bet anything their house is being surveilled, too," Mike replied.

"And their phone?"

"That, too. If we could get these diaries into the Zone, we could ship them back to the states somehow."

The next few weeks were filled with doubt and fear for all of us. I had two weeks remaining at the NCO Academy. Marie was doing laundry in our apartment one afternoon when the buzzer for the security door at the bottom of the stairs sounded, making her jump.

"Immigration. Open the door, please," demanded a thickly accented male voice over the intercom.

Marie froze momentarily. A tidal wave of hopelessness swept over her. Thoughts of the school's cover story about volunteer services raced through her mind. Reaching for the button by the door, she hesitated, then pushed it, letting the caller in.

The man was very polite, offering what appeared at first glance to be proper credentials, and asking questions that a census taker would. He was impeccably dressed in a white cotton breza shirt, black slacks, and Gucci shoes. Never volunteering any personal information, and remaining cautious about mentioning anything about my whereabouts, or relationships with any of our neighbors, Marie carefully maintained eye contact with the strange little man. Still having doubts about the real purpose for the surprise visit, Marie stayed within close proximity of her only means of defense, besides a practiced knee to the groin---a heavy brass candlestick holder resting on the bookshelf by the front door.

Something was very wrong, Marie thought. As if mentally photographing the layout of the apartment, the man glanced around, moving quickly from room to room, as if searching for something to incriminate the occupants. Eying a basket of laundry on top of the washer near the kitchen door, he strolled over to where Marie was nervously folding clothes. He reached in front of Marie, picking up a cotton bra from the basket, and held it up, smiling lewdly at Marie. Then it was on.

"That's it, you phony son-of-a-bitch!" she snarled, grabbing for the candlestick. "Get your skinny ass out of here before they have to carry you out!" Out the door and down the steps he ran, mumbling to himself in Spanish.

The following day, I was notified of the incident by the Senior Tactical NCO at the academy. Fearing for Marie's safety, I was allowed to call her immediately. Marie was always a strong person, and played the whole thing down, saying that Mike had done everything possible, and for me not to worry. Mike arranged to have a warrant sworn for the man's arrest.

A lineup at the National Police headquarters had done nothing to allay Marie's fears; they were only magnified. Being led down a flight of stairs into a large, well-lit room, She stood in full view of four suspects. The man identifying himself as an immigration official was standing in the lineup, grinning venomously at Marie.

"It had to have been a setup," Mike deduced. "This knucklehead must have been sent to your place to look around."

"Now I know we're being watched! The sooner we get those diaries into the Zone, the better," Marie conceded.

In the days that followed, Marie went up my chain-of-command, embarrassing some, yet getting help from others, finally managing to acquire family quarters for us in the Canal Zone. Cocoli, a substandard housing area just west of the Miraflores Locks, wasn't much to look at, but it would offer adequate and safer living conditions. These tropical style quarters were condemned by the U.S. Navy in 1948, then taken over by the Army and refurbished for family housing. The temporary quarters would offer a secure hiding place for the collection of diaries written by Dr. Schumann. Hidden carefully in cases of books and magazines, the diaries were transported to the storeroom of our new apartment.

The Schumann family was at last reunited, then exiled to Sweden---an agreement the Torrijos regime made in exchange for a written statement by Dr. Schumann never to show his face in Panama again, nor write another subversive word on Latin American politics.

The diaries filtered out of the country one-by-one through the APO, eventually finding their way to Sweden, and into the hands of the author. A source of fear and intrigue for Marie and I, the Perkins', and the Schumanns, was at last laid to rest.

Panama was not all danger and espionage, however. Contrasting with the grim outlook of the past several months, more attractive and simpler diversions were available. The ruins of Old Panama, brought alive with folkloric festivals held within its monolithic walls, the gothic Cathedral of Panama, the Thatcher Ferry Bridge back-dropped by Ancon Hill and the Port of Balboa, and an endless list of places of interest all added to the contrasting beauty of Panama. Unceasing photo opportunities made this tiny nation even more inviting.

Boquete was a 'city of flowers', nestled in the fertile Baru volcanic region. Roughly a four hour drive from Panama City, the flower capital of Panama offered a brief refuge from the crush of the city. With small town charm, shops, restaurants, and family-owned hotels lined the main street in the middle of town.

Marie and I registered at a small hotel on the edge of town. Although the owner's choice of colors, a hideous combination of aquamarine and pink, didn't exactly match our tastes, the hotel was clean and inviting. One and two bedroom cabins rimmed the hillside behind the main building. A spring-fed stream meandering between the buildings with flagstone walkways romantically illuminated with Japanese lanterns enhanced the quiet charm and peaceful setting of this great weekend getaway.

Back in the Canal Zone, life didn't take very long to get back the normal daily grind. My job at the photo lab in Corozal demanded long hours, including some weekends. On-call tours of duty were rotated a week at a time between all the photographers. Late night calls from CID or MP investigators often turned into an all night affair.

"Six-Three, this is Five-Six, over," the code for the Staff Duty NCO calling for photo support crackled over the Motorola on the night stand.

"Six-Three, go ahead," I croaked, rubbing sleep from my eyes and looking at the clock. Two in the morning.

"Six-Three, give Lewis a call at CID," came the instructions from the SDNCO.

Special Agent Lewis was on call with the Regional CID office this week. I always hated having duty when he was on call. Everything from a crab and shark-bitten floater washing up on some desolate beach, to a drug raid in one of the barracks seemed to be normal fare. I dialed Lewis' number and let it ring while I cleared my throat.

"Hi, this is Smitty," I said, still sleepily stumbling over my words. "What's up?"

"Mornin," Lewis greeted in his normal Okie drawl. "Meet me at the office and we'll drive over to Clayton. Got lucky on an H and W tonight." H and W was short for health and welfare inspection of the barracks, commonly referred to as a drug raid.

Lewis parked the new unmarked Ford Galaxy behind the Mechanized Infantry barracks at Clayton, next to the mess hall loading dock. Any unmarked police car could be identified a mile away because of their simplicity and the single FM antenna protruding from the roof.

After shooting a small, but career-destroying cache of drugs found in a wall locker and the guilty party in custody, Lewis and I walked back to the car. Freezing in his tracks, he stopped and stared at the new Ford, mouth agape and speechless.

"Aw shit!" he was finally able to blurt out.

Evidently, someone Lewis had made enemies with in the past had retaliated on behalf of a friend busted in the raid that night. A high pressure water hose was leading from the wash rack near the loading dock through an open rear window of the new sedan. Over a foot of water was standing inside the car, laying waste to the interior.

Trying very hard to keep from busting out laughing, I simply pointed out to the infuriated Lewis, still in shock from the embarrassing discovery, that maybe we should have locked the car. He didn't appreciate my observation, or my sense of humor.

Aside from crime scene photography and studio work, the skills of an Army photographer were called on periodically by the Public Affairs Office. The inner offices of the white, tropical-style building next to the Southern Command Headquarters at Quarry Heights buzzed with the activity of a newspaper copy room. Typewriters clacked out the latest stories of military and political achievements of the region. A small, but functional darkroom in the corner of the office area served as my temporary office.

I was busy printing some old black and white negatives I'd brought in that morning, when Herb Ellersby's unmistakable, nasal voice came over the intercom.

"Smitty, got an assignment for you. Grab your camera and go to the CinC's office in fifteen minutes for a shoot." Herb was editor-in-chief of the Pan Canal Press, the weekly public information newspaper in the Zone. His sense of urgency with even the slightest things made people jump.

"On the way, sir," I replied, grabbing the loaded Mimiya six by seven and a battery pack for the strobe on the way out the door.

Building One was only a short city block from the PAO. Unfortunately, during the rainy season, time and distance had no merit. As if by fate or perfect timing, I ran smack-dab into a wall of rain halfway between the two buildings, totally destroying the starched freshness of my khakis.

Getting no more than a sympathetic look from the MP at the guard desk, I ran up the stairs to the CinC's office, leaving a trail of wet shoe prints all the way. As I walked into the outer office, General William

Rosson, the Commander-in-Chief of the Southern Command stepped out of his office to speak to his aide. He regarded my soaked uniform with disbelief. Had I not photographed General Rosson on several occasions, sharing a professional rapport, I would have been terrified.

"Specialist Smith, what the Sam Hill did you fall into?" the General asked in that undeniable booming voice, with a broad smile spreading across his face. General Rosson stood over six-three. His rugged muscular features, deep-set eyes, and gravely voice were sufficient to strike terror in the hearts of brave men, much less a sopping wet photographer.

"Sorry about that, sir," I replied sheepishly. "Got caught in the rain."

With a grin and a nod, as quickly as he'd emerged from his office, the CinC turned to finish the conversation with his aide.

When the shoot, nothing more than a routine award presentation, was completed, I headed back to the PAO to develop the film and give the finished prints to Herb. The midday sun was blazing down, causing plumes of steam to rise off the wet pavement.

Over the next several months, Marie and I enrolled in some courses at the Canal Zone College in Balboa. Feeling strange to again be a part of the academic grind, we both adjusted easily to that old familiar environment. It was actually fun this time. Classes like English Lit and American History were interspersed with hands-on electives like Photojournalism and Audio-Visual Techniques. Maturity and self discipline were now vital parts of my life, and my grades showed a drastic improvement from those in the past.

The entire Panama experience created new horizons for us. Lessons learned at the NCO Academy would carry throughout the rest of my military career. Initially, the dreamy notion of needing to be in a combat arms MOS (Military Occupational Specialty) in order to apply the concepts of leadership, methods of instruction, map reading, and field tactics was very common. Later on, I realized that learning those skills and more was just as important in any job in the Army. Words from the past echoed in my mind: *Rely on your training,* and *...Never lose your sense of humor, no matter what happens.*

One of those times when a sick sense of humor seemed the only rational alternative to going stark raving mad, Mike Perkins was getting out of the Army, and he and Barb were scheduled to leave the next day, Nixon resigned in the face of the Watergate scandal, and our old Datsun blew a head gasket, leaving me stranded on the way to take a final exam at

Canal Zone College. Things could have been worse, I supposed. Oh yeah, it was raining buckets that afternoon.

'Going back to the world' was a special time everyone on an overseas tour waited for with great anticipation. The end of our three year tour in Panama was close at hand. In order to extend to three years, Marie had to fly out of Panama, get her visa stamped in Costa Rica, then reenter Panama, then I could apply for command sponsorship. In the meantime, I had gotten promoted to SP5 and boarded for SSG shortly thereafter.

Aberdeen Proving Grounds, Maryland, would be our next stop. Once again, plans and arrangements were set in motion for a new home, another way and place to meet new friends. An Army family for nearly five years, Marie and I regarded ourselves as pros in the moving game. Home was where the Army sent us. Looking back on the past three years, our emotions ran from anticipating an exciting new adventure to longing to remain with close friends in a known environment. We'd gone down that uncharted road several times in the past together, and we'd do it again. And again.

11. Transition

My newest assignment was to Delta Company, 519th Military Intelligence Battalion at Aberdeen Proving Grounds in January '75. The small, but vital unit was detached from a battalion at Ft Bragg, North Carolina. Delta's responsibility was to receive, refurbish, maintain and ultimately distribute Soviet Tanks, artillery, small arms, and electronics equipment seized in the Arab-Israeli War, to U.S Army units world-wide for the purpose of Opposing Forces (OPFOR) training. Part of my job was to photograph these tanks and other vehicles inside and out, and set up studio shoots of weapons, radio equipment and uniforms worn by soviet soldiers. Following the photo process, operator's and maintenance manuals to accompany all equipment being shipped out were assembled in our drafting section.

Over the years, I had gained a vast resume of photographic experience from medical photography, to extensive studio portraiture, public affairs and information work, to industrial photography, which was the consideration at APG. All these accolades, however offered little help or hope of being promoted to Staff Sergeant. Each passing month, I would closely scrutinize the posted promotion list, and bug the stew out of folks at the personnel office in hopes of learning more ways of gaining extra promotion points, to no avail. Set back and be patient was always the response.

Since patience was never a virtue of mine, I tendered some of the reasons that I wasn't meeting promotion criteria. Ever a proud soldier, I'd always tried to do and look my best. Primary Leadership development Course (PLDC) and the NCO Academy, completed in Panama. College credits, correspondence courses and letters of commendation from superiors depicting achievements above and beyond all sat quietly unnoticed in my personnel records. The rationale was that a limited number of soldiers were promoted monthly to selected grades in MOS's needing a predetermined number of soldiers in that higher grade. However easy that logic was to understand, I had trouble accepting it.

Another possibility of an unforeseen promotion could have been related to a rather humorous incident that took place a few moths prior. At a company barbeque, a Second Lieutenant new to Delta Company was engaged in a beer fight with some NCO's. Marie and I were relaxing at a picnic table talking and playing with our new baby girl, Allison, lying in a carrier on the table. After getting showered with beer, I yelled at the raucous group to be a little more careful. No sooner did I get that out of my system, another hail of cold beer hit the three of us. Taking off after the young LT, I chased him down a steep hill into some trees, launching a flying tackle, landing on top of the guy, driving him into the ground with my knee in his back and his face in the dirt, knocking the wind out of his sails. Thought I'd killed the poor guy, because he just laid there. Shortly, he began groaning and sputtering.

Shocked by my own impulsive actions of attacking an officer and seeing the remote possibility of getting promoted becoming even more unattainable, I extended my hand to help him to his feet. We both apologized to each other, becoming good friends after that.

As a result of that momentary lapse in judgement, 2LT Frank Canton, a newly commissioned ROTC graduate from the University of Virginia, was given a stinging Officer Efficiency Report. A bad OER for a new officer while still in the probationary phase of his or her first assignment was likened to career suicide. Unless Frank had a very compassionate and understanding commander further down the road, I doubted if he ever saw First Lieutenant.

My sentence, however, was a little lighter. Conduct unbecoming of an NCO was the comment placed in my Non-commissioned Officer's Efficiency Report, which followed me for years to come. Everyone in Delta Company got a big chuckle out of the fracas, except the company commander, a hard-bitten Major and Vietnam veteran. He read me the riot act when he called me in to his office to sign the fateful NCOER. No sense of humor. I, on the other hand, earned the distinction of being the guy who tried to squash a butter bar like a bug.

Still contemplating the elusive E6 stripes, I was given a training manual for Air Traffic Control Procedures to look over by a fellow NCO who worked in the drafting and illustrating section. We'd talked extensively in the past about ATC and possibilities of a quicker promotion. I'd been a photographer for eight years, and thoroughly enjoyed the diversity it had to offer, but I was thinking in economic terms at that point. A promotion to Staff Sergeant would mean about a two-hundred dollar a month pay increase.

"Check it out," SSG Russ Henderson offered. I have an old friend in ATC, he says promotions aren't too bad. He really likes it. Right now, he's in Korea, but he's got orders for Bragg. Just look over the TM and go see Olson at personnel and fill out a 4187 for an MOS change. Couldn't hurt to try."

Marie and I were on a two weeks' leave at her folks' place in Melbourne when the call came through from SFC Olson, NCOIC of records back at APG. I'd received reassignment orders for the ATC School at Ft. Rucker.

"Your report date to Rucker is 3 August," SFC Olson said. "You need to head back as soon as you can and start clearing post no later than 13 July."

That was on Saturday, 8 July. I had a quick decision to make; one that would again affect the whole family. Marie worked as a nurse at a clinic near Aberdeen, and Allison was about thirteen months old. We'd discussed the job change at length, and were expecting orders. Not while we were on leave, however. Baby Allison was very flexible---she went where Mommy and Daddy went. Marie would have to put in a short notice when we got back to APG.

"You know we just bought the trailer," Marie reasoned. "We'll have to sell it or move it. What about our friends?" I could tell by her reaction Marie would not be in full support of this move. Up until now, reassignments were the luck of the draw. This one, I requested.

Cutting short our stay with Marie's parents, we packed up and headed back to Maryland, discussing, rationalizing, and planning our next move the whole trip back. This would be another chapter in our lives, but one not as painless and trouble free as others.

By the time we arrived back in Maryland, the plan was set.---the Army would contract a trailer moving company to haul our mobile home to Alabama and we'd say goodbye to our friends. Army families did that. Moves to a new post every two or three years taught us how to say goodbye, pack up a house or give away what we never used or needed, and meet new friends wherever the Army sent us.

Clearing post was completed, all papers signed, TA-50 field gear was cleaned and turned in. It was all over but the shouting. I only needed to sign out of Delta Company, and we'd be on our way to Alabama. The Army Finance office at Rucker informed me that Uncle Sam would only pay seventy-five cents on the dollar to move a trailer. Interstate fuel permits, and unexpected expenses on the road would be our responsibility, payable at the end of the line. Well, I wanted a career change, but I had to also accept the ramifications that came with it. We'd make it through. We always did.

The driver for the trailer moving company arrived one morning the day after I'd finished clearing post. He was driving an old Ford cab-over he'd found in a junk yard and restored it.

"She may not look like much," he conceded, "but she runs good."

I was standing in the street looking at that primer gray hulk waiting to snatch my home out of its resting place and haul it off to our new home in Alabama. Walking around the old truck, I was admittedly impressed. The truck was setting in the street idling with the throaty rumble of a cammed-up big block V8. The frame and entire undercarriage was painted a glistening black. New tires were installed making the old truck look entirely road-worthy.

The driver set to the task, with little wasted motion, of getting the mobile home ready for the road. Unanchored, unblocked, and ready to be hitched up to the truck, we hit another snag. Four of the six tires on the trailer were badly weather checked and needed to be replaced. Ka-ching! It continued. More expenses. We knew this wouldn't be easy.

With the new tires on the trailer, the driver slowly pulled it off the lot, heading down the down the street towards I-95. The old Ford hauled the heavy, sixty foot load with ease. Marie and I watched as our home disappeared out of sight, hoping we'd strategically packed all the heavy furniture amidships to properly distribute the weight over the axles, knowing it had been checked and rechecked.

The car was packed and ready for the trip. The cranberry and white '74 Cutlass was given a quick trip check at a local garage. The next morning, Allison was securely buckled into her car seat, and the three of us headed south on our journey to Alabama.

Morning traffic on the Beltway around DC was light, but steady. It was smooth sailing. For a while. A few miles south of Washington, I spotted a trailer house sitting alongside the busy highway, listing precariously to the right. The closer we came to the crippled behemoth, the more it resembled our trailer. Pulling off the road behind it, we recognized it as our mobile home. Mouth agape, I speechlessly looked at Marie. She was returning my stare with tear-filled eyes.

"We'll get through this," I comforted her, wondering how we were going to accomplish that. "I'll go check and see if he left a note."

A quick walk around of the disabled trailer revealed that two of the three curbside tires had blown, shearing the electric brakes down to the axles and causing the trailer to list dangerously to the right. Tire and brake debris scattered along the shoulder and roadway for several hundred feet. Locating the door key, I crawled in the front door past the packed boxes of clothes and household goods to check for any damage inside. Fortunately, everything was intact, just as we had packed it.

Back on the road heading south, Marie and I sat in silence for several hours. We were both deep in thought about solutions to the dilemma we faced.

We were only a few hours from Augusta, Georgia, the home of old friends Vince and Helen Broderick, who had moved there from Aberdeen two years earlier.

Vince was a retired Master Sergeant who headed up the Communications and Electronics (C&E) section back at Delta Company. He owned a small air conditioning and heating repair business in Augusta. We stopped at a gas station outside of Augusta to call them letting them know about the disaster that had beset us, asking if we could camp out in their living room until we could find out what the status of the trailer was. Pay phones were the order of the day if you didn't have a CB radio, and of course cell phones weren't in existence.

When we arrived at Vince and Helen's place about eight o'clock that night, there was a wonderful home cooked meal waiting for us, as well as comfort for three weary travelers. Allison, naturally, slept through the whole ordeal, appearing to care nothing about anything except a meal of mashed peas and apricots and a clean diaper.

Phone calls were made to the carrier's home office in Oklahoma City concerning the status of our abandoned, broken-down trailer and the whereabouts of the driver.

"Ken had some problems on the road with your unit," the dispatcher was very apologetic for our inconvenience.

"Where is he now?"

"He had to drive up to Pennsylvania to pick up some brake parts and tires, saying he'd be back on the road no later than tomorrow afternoon. As a matter of fact, he just called to say he's back working on the trailer. He should be able to meet you at Ft Rucker late Thursday afternoon."

Thank God. Problem solved. That part, anyway. Unspeakable visions go through a person's mind when he sees everything he owns sitting alongside a busy highway, and no one's around to tell you what happened.

Parked along and access road outside the east gate at Ft Rucker Thursday afternoon around 4:30, Marie and I sat patiently waiting to see our house being hauled down the road. Everything was set. I'd completed most of the in-processing on post, and had signed for a lot at the post trailer park. Allison was cooing in the back seat munching on a box of raisins.

My excitement rose as I glanced in the rearview mirror to see the primer gray truck with our trailer in tow looming up behind us. Finally, things were looking up from what they were a few days ago south of DC on the side of the road.

Greeting the driver, I briefed him on how I would lead him across Ft Rucker to the trailer park on the west side. It was nearly four miles from where we sat outside the east gate. Ken looked exhausted after his cross-country trek, yet he insisted on telling all about his event-filled trip down from Maryland. I responded in kind by adding how thankful I was to see the house in one piece. Again.

The rag-tag caravan of a loaded-down dirty red Cutlass and a hulking gray truck hauling a sixty foot trailer pulled slowly into the post trailer park. Always a novelty for the kids that lived there, a trailer house being towed slowly down the street needed an escort, so a small group on their bicycles began to follow us to our assigned lot.

Stopping in front of lot Sixty Three, Ken began the surgical process of backing the long trailer painstakingly between a pine tree and the concrete patio. Perfect fit. Expert driving, except a side mirror was lost to the unforgiving pine tree.

Life as an Air Traffic Control student at Ft Rucker was anything but mundane. Early morning formations, followed by the road marches that would take us to the old classroom buildings at the bottom of Tank Hill would be an important part of the daily routine. Part of the original Camp Rucker dating back to the days of World War II, the old buildings on Tank Hill were slowly being demolished, giving way to more modern facilities on the main part of the post.

Before my classes began on 8 August, I was assigned to a student company for work details. 'Casual', they called it. My squad leader, Roger Burton, was a hard-stripe E5 with a little over three years in the service. I was a Spec 5 with almost eight years in grade. I kept reminding myself of the sole reason I dragged my family to Ft Rucker, was a promotion to Staff Sergeant.

Sgt Burton was all spit and polish, but had very limited people skills, and was even less of a leader of men. But, he was still in charge by virtue of the buck sergeant stripes. He barked orders at everyone in the squad: *"Go there, get that, come here, do this."* He simply parroted orders from the First Sergeant, rather than paraphrasing and interpreting, and leading by example. Guys like that had little leadership experience, and were labeled 'Shake-n-Bakes.' It got pretty old. All I ever said to him was, "Yes, Sarge."

During roll call formation on a sunny September morning, two other soldiers and I were called to the front of the formation to report to the commander. The three of us were promoted in front of the student company that day---the other two guys to Spec 4, and I to Staff Sergeant. Wow! I didn't see that coming. I hadn't been following the promotion list for weeks, and didn't have the slightest idea I was being promoted that day, and I was positive Sgt Burton didn't either, judging from the look of dismay on his face.

Dismissed by the CO, I marched smartly back to the first squad, standing face to face with Burton. "Sgt Burton, move out to the end of the squad," was all I said to him. I saw by his expression, that he wouldn't like what was coming.

SP5's with eight years in grade are like old warrant officers. You don't mess with either one of them. Young Sgt Burton turned into a blithering yes-man, always by my side wanting to know if he could do anything for me; squad details or rat out a squad member for not doing his job. For a short while, I had him lead the afternoon PT formations and police calls around the barracks. I tried instilling some better people skills in him by having him talk to the guys, getting to know them a little better, before busting right in and demanding their respect. That worked a little to help him become a better leader. But at times, I just wanted to say to him, "Look, you idiot, that's not the way to do it!"

Basic academics and non-radar approach control classes were taught in the classrooms on tank Hill. Non-radar was far and above the most exasperating and difficult part of the course. Many would-be controllers washed out of this part of the course and were reclassified into different MOS's. Having a lot at stake, I spent many late nights with my nose in training and technical manuals, and at the post Learn Center going through an endless supply of video quizzes on ATC procedures.

Hard work ultimately paid off when I was passed on to Kelly Hall, the advanced part of the ATC School. Working in tower and radar simulator classrooms after taking quizzes hour after hour on Tank Hill was like transitioning from high school to college. Every procedure I learned before was put to the test in the simulators.

Upon graduating from ATC School, I was assigned to Hanchey Army Airfield, an initial entry training field for the helicopter flight school, at Rucker. Sarah, our youngest, came into the world just after I started working at Hanchey. She would grow to be wrapped around Daddy's little finger. I was the new kid on the block for a while until other controllers came from the school or other assignments somewhere in the world. I was treated to all the initiation rites any other 'cherry' was subjected to.

"Go down to Base Ops and get five hundred yards of flight line."

"Call Cairns and ask for the approach gate key. Tell 'em you'll pick it up in thirty minutes."

"Get a bucket of rotor wash from maintenance."

Most of the time, I simply smiled and nodded. I recall a time when a young controller was sent to Ops for a length of flight line, and was shuffled from building to building on the airfield on a well-choreographed search for the elusive rope. Everyone from the ATC Chief, to base Ops, and even the flight training office was in on that one.

Six helicopter parking lane lanes on the west side of Hanchey Tower were dedicated to initial entry trainers, the old Hughes TH-55's with reciprocating engines. A pilot and copilot sat side by side inside the glass bubble. Controllers dubbed the misshapen aircraft the 'Bumble Bee', because that's what it looked and sounded like. These birds were also used for solo flights for student pilots earning their paper wings. The six parking lanes on the east side of the tower were use for Hueys, Cobras, and Chinooks, all part of advanced flight training.

One bright, chilly November morning, I was working ground and local control on the west side, when a Bumble Bee called for taxi instructions.

"Hanchey Ground, Army 687, lane four for taxi to the pad," the shrill, nervous voice of a solo student pilot came over the mike.

"Army 687, Hanchey Ground, taxi to the pad, wind calm, altimeter two niner niner seven, over," I responded, trying to calm the young student pilot down a bit.

No response.

"Army 687, do you copy?" I asked.

Another delay. "Army 687, roger, taxi to the pad." He was probably didn't want to admit that he was scared, or he was busy reading his "How to Fly This Thing" book.

With several jerky motions, as if trying to maintain collective and pedal coordination, he finally hovered out of the parallel parking of acres of parked trainers to a safe spot in the middle of the taxi lane. For what seemed like an eternity, after several seconds, he was on the move again. Moments like this, you don't take your eyes off the aircraft you're talking to.

"Hanchey Tower, Army 687 pad four for a south departure."

"Army 687, Hanchey, wind clam, cleared for takeoff."

Another delay. No response. Gradually, 687 came to an unsteady hover, swaying back and forth at about six feet. After a few seconds doing that crazy dance, he spun around two or three times, then landed back on the pad with what had to have been a bone-shattering crunch.

"Army 687, are you alright? Do you wish to declare an emergency?" I asked, being cautious how and when I keyed the mike in order to mask the raucous laughter coming from the tower cab.

"Negative, Hanchey, must have some loose fan belts," came the reply. Poor guy was probably embarrassed to tears, hoping his IP wasn't watching the performance.

"Roger, Army 687, advise ready." More laughter from the tower.

More delay. "Hanchey, Army 687 ready for departure."

"687, cleared for takeoff." Good luck, my man, I thought to myself, watching him closely as he pulled pitch, taking off to the south.

More laughter and guffaws arose from the tower cab. The other controllers were in stitches as they laughed and waved at the poor guy, still dancing and wavering in the distance.

"OHR! OHR! Somebody give Smith an OHR form so he can write that guy up for wanting to be a pilot!" An OHR was an Operational Hazard Report that was entered into a pilot's or controller's file for an unsafe act. That was the first OHR I'd written. I really had no choice. I thought the other controllers were joking, but theoretically, the pilot was seen as a danger to himself and others.

January '80 was fast approaching. My current enlistment would be up the first part of February. Marie and I had been talking about re-upping for Hawaii, so I started getting with the reenlistment NCO at Cairns about a possible slot. Unfortunately, talking to that guy turned out to be a real turn-off.

Sergeant First Class Ronald Kean, the re-up NCO, was less than helpful about encouraging me to reenlist. I wanted to in the worst way, but he was as much help as putting a milk pail under a bull.

"You wouldn't like Hawaii," he said. "I've been there, and besides, there aren't any slots right now."

"How about checking with DA? I asked, impatiently. You don't tell a doctor or fellow NCO how to do his job. You suggest it subliminally.

"I already have. How about Germany? There're plenty of slots there."

"No thanks," I replied, walking out of his office.

Discouraged and fed up with incompetent NCOs, I decided to let it go and leave the Army at the end of January. Marie supported that decision, but it would mean another move. We'd also have to sell the trailer, after having paid the twelve hundred dollars back to the Army for the move from Maryland.

Well, that was that. We sold the trailer, and Marie took the girls and went back to Iowa. I had just finished processing out, so I thought I'd go out to Hanchey and say goodbye to friends and coworkers. Sergeant Major Lee, NCOIC of the ATC Branch at USACC (US Army Communications Command), called the tower looking for me.

"Sergeant Smith, I've got two slots in Hawaii for you, which one do you want?" his voice boomed through the receiver. SGM Lee was a huge, boisterous man whose voice increased by several decibels when he got excited. His voice was getting louder.

"Sergeant Major," I tried to pick my words carefully, "your man at Cairns told me there were no slots and that I wouldn't like Hawaii anyway because he'd been there. I believe that if everyone involved were excited about me reenlisting last month as you are now, and if Kean had done his job, I'd have stayed and reenlisted." Right then, I felt I'd just stepped in it.

"Now Smith," the Sergeant Major continued tactfully, "we can change all that with a stroke of the pen. You don't have to get out," he pleaded.

"Sergeant Major, you don't understand. I've already sold my house, my hold baggage was picked up last week, and my family is in Iowa. I'm done."

"Well, sorry we can't change all that for you. Sure hate to lose you, but if you're ever back this way, stop in and see us," he offered. Not bloody likely, I thought to myself.

Marie had rented a small frame house back in Melbourne. When she showed up in town with the girls, and not me, the town gossips' tongues began to wag.

"Oh, those poor little girls!" they'd say. "Look at them, the poor dears, he just up and left them."

Marie and her folks got quite a chuckle out of all the talking going on. In a small town, where everyone knows everybody else's business, things like this often get blown out of proportion. Marie knew exactly when I'd be in town, and laughingly prepared me for all the idle talk going on. Allison and Sarah knew when to expect Daddy, too.

When I arrived in Melbourne, I felt as if I'd left a part of me behind. Not Ft Rucker, but the Army. The military had been a big part of our lives for ten years. We were on our own without the benefit of having family nearby. It was good to be back home, but it wouldn't seem the same. Marie's folks lived there in Melbourne, and so did one of my older sisters, Bette, and her husband. About four years earlier, my parents had bought a small house in Marshalltown, about twenty minutes east, off Highway 30.

Switching roles completely, Marie landed a fulltime nursing job in Marshalltown, and I became Mr. Mom. I'd bundle the kids up in their snowsuits, and pull them uptown on the sled to visit old friends, or shop for a few groceries at a family-owned market. The girls and I had a lot of fun spending time together; baking cookies, building snowmen, keeping up our small house, and reading children's books. Our days were pretty well filled up.

In the meantime, I had joined the National Guard unit in Marshalltown, just to keep in touch with the military. Part of a signal battalion, the unit was comprised of pole climbers, switchboard operators, and radio and teletype operators, commonly known as RATT Riggers.

My first drill weekend, I strolled proudly into the armory in my starched fatigues and spit-shined jump boots, looking around and sizing up the place and its weekend warriors. Some guys looked as if they'd slept in their fatigues, and never introduced Mr. Kiwi to their boots. Others were relaxing on couches in the dayroom, while still others played cards. Feeling slightly out of my element with my fresh-from-the-regular Army look in this slack outfit, I looked around for the Orderly Room.

Rocky Templeton, a short, stocky roughneck I used to run with in high school, was now the First Sergeant of Bravo Company, 114th Signal Battalion. He walked up to me, smiling and greeting me like an old friend. Rocky had been on the police force in town for the past ten years. He was the last person I'd suspect of pursuing a career in law enforcement. We had some wild times in high school.

Rocky joined the Guard about the same time, and proceeded up the leadership ladder.

"Be careful around here," he cautioned, "this ain't the Army." He noticed me making a few uniform corrections on my way in.

"Roger that, point taken," I said apologetically.

"We do things a little differently here. I'll give you a full briefing after formation."

Later on, after all the necessary 'new guy' paperwork was completed in the orderly room, Rocky gave me the grand tour, introducing me to men of the unit, and the guys I'd be working closely with. I was being assigned to the switchboard, a Korean War relic installed in a converted deuce-and-a half shop van. Cords and jacks. Millions of them. It was pretty overwhelming.

Break time rolled around at 0900. This meant a group discussion was held to decide who would drive to the donut shop, almost clear across the town of about 48,000. By the time the gopher, not me, by the way, returned with the donuts, nearly an hour had passed. I realized that the clock on break time didn't actually start until the donuts arrived. After that, the only thing anticipated of any importance was lunch and the 1300 formation. Boy, Rocky sure hit the nail on the head.

By the time the third drill weekend rolled around, I'd just about made up my mind to plunge back into full time Army life. I had been on a futile job search since coming back to Melbourne. The unemployment checks were adequate, but it just wasn't the same. I simply didn't belong.

In April of 1980, Co B, 114th Signal Battalion participated in annual training at Ft Gordon, Georgia. We were flown by C-130 from the Air National Guard field at the Des Moines airport, making me feel I was back in my comfort zone.

Ft Gordon was a sprawling Army post outside of Augusta, near the South Carolina state line. Red Georgia clay hills and sugar pine stands surrounded the newer brick buildings, and the WWII era structures still standing as a constant reminder of what a military installation looked and felt like.

Over the course of the next two weeks, I was to absorb all I could about the operation and maintenance of the switchboard. However, my frame of mind was to reenlist in the Army upon my return to Marshalltown. The National Guard was not for me. After a while, the instructors at Gordon began to sound like Charlie Brown's teacher. Nothing seemed to register. All I heard were muffled voices.

Back in Marshalltown, I made regular visits to the recruiter's office. I didn't take a lot of convincing on my part, though the recruiter had a tough time breaking my contract with the 114th. But after making few phone calls, calling in markers from old friends, he was successful. As per regulations, I would lose one pay grade coming back to active duty. Ironically, however, the only place with available slots for my grade and MOS was Ft Rucker. I just hoped that SGM Lee had forgotten how unprofessional I was with him back in January.

Only minutes before the recruiter arrived in Melbourne to take me to Des Moines to be to be sworn in, I received a phone call from Fisher Governor Company, a major employer in Marshalltown. They wanted to schedule an interview for the drafting and illustrating section of the R&D Department. The timing was way off, and I had to refuse their offer. About a month earlier, I'd have grabbed the opportunity for employment. At this point, I knew I'd made the right decision for my family and me.

Go time was near. My new report date to Rucker was 21 May, and today was 6 May. The packers were due in just a few short days. By now, Marie and I were old hands at packing and moving, but experience had taught us that no two moves were the same.

Saying our goodbyes at a two-family gathering, my parents didn't understand why we couldn't make a move back home work, but Marie's folks recognized the fact our self-sufficiency over the years had been hard-won. Additionally, in nearly ten years of marriage, the Army was all we knew.

12. Back to Ft Rucker

It was a beautiful spring Iowa morning, with the temperature in the low sixties. The morning sun was bursting over the corn fields on the east side of town. At 0600, we were packed and ready to hit the road. This time, though, there were two cars and a motorcycle in the caravan. Marie had purchased a '71 Olds Delta 88 as a second car. What a land yacht! I dubbed it the 'Brown Bomber.' A month ago, I bought a Suzuki 550 to cruise around on. Of course, I needed a trailer to haul it on, so I picked up a used utility trailer and bolted a bike-hauling track on it, and had a hitch installed on the Brown Bomber. Marie would be behind the wheel of our year old black Cutlass Supreme. With a forty channel CB installed in each car, we had two way communication for moral support on the long trip to Alabama. Marie, being the better navigator of the two of us, could quickly tell me if I made a wrong turn.

Not wanting to drive day and night like in our earlier days, we pulled into a Motel-6 in Paducah, Kentucky, after a grueling twelve hours on the road. Allison was fast asleep in her car seat in the back seat of the Bomber, and Sarah was in the same state of slumber in the back of the Cutlass. It seemed a shame to wake them, but after carrying them both gently into our temporary home on the road and tucking them in on one of the queen-sized beds, they were both sleeping soundly again in minutes.

Exhausted at the end of the first leg of our trip back to Rucker, Marie and I laid in bed, talking about returning to army life; how we'd both missed it in the past few months.

"Let's try and get into quarters this time," Marie commented. "The waiting list can't be that long since we'd been gone."

"Sounds like a plan," I agreed. "You remember Chris Hayes, and uh, what was his wife's name? They had the little boy that Allison tried to beat up for pushing Sarah in the swing. Their place was sort of small, but it was pretty nice."

"I know, but if we could get in there, we could save a little and put some money away for a house someday." Marie was a planner and a manager, and I always found it prudent to listen to her ideas.

"When we get to Rucker, I'll get on the housing list when I process in," I said sleepily. It had been a long day, but our minds were racing with thoughts of returning to army life, family housing, and the new job.

"Good night, Babe, let's try and get some rest," I said drowsily. "Love you." We kissed goodnight, rolled over back to back, and nestled down for some much-needed sleep.

Around 5:30 that afternoon, we rolled into Ozark, thankful the long trip was over. Personnel wouldn't be open until early the next day, so we checked into a hotel, then went to get a bite to eat at Captain D's. Ozark was a small, but thriving city outside of Rucker's east gate. Marie worked as a floor nurse at the Dale County Hospital in town until a few months ago, and Sarah was born there in April of last year.

Morning came with another bright sun streaming through the tall pines surrounding the hotel. I kissed Marie and the girls goodbye.

"I'll be back around noon and we'll get some lunch. Love you, Babe. Love you, too, guys."

"Love you, Daddy, have fun at the Army," Sarah and Allison chimed in unison. Sarah didn't have much of a vocabulary yet, but she knew 'Love you, Daddy.'

A ten minute drive to main post began the long day of in processing… again. Along the way to the personnel office, the old familiar post brought back memories…some good, some bad. I felt that I was back home. Air traffic control students and warrant officer candidates were standing proudly in formation outside of Kelly Hall along the main drag, ready to begin another day of academics in the classrooms and simulators.

Seeing a lot of familiar faces at the USACC (US Army Communications Command) personnel office, I began the task of processing in. One bright spot was that SGM Lee was on terminal leave, pending retirement. I was relieved to learn he was no longer a threat to me or any assignment I'd draw.

Stage Field Branch had placed me at High Bluff Stage Field, about twelve miles south of Enterprise. Johnny Edison, High Bluff's assistant facility chief, happened to be in the office taking care of facility business. We met when I was a controller at Hanchey. Johnny was working as a controller at Highbluff at the time, and we became friends at company gatherings. We often pulled CQ (Charge of Quarters) together at the company orderly room at Cairns Army Airfield. Johnny was a well-educated and respected young black Staff Sergeant on his way up the career chain.

"Great seeing you again, Smythe." He always called me that, but it never bothered me.

"How's it goin', Jay?" I returned.

"Welcome back. You ready to work? I see you got on out at High Bluff. You'll like it, being away from the flagpole. It can get pretty busy out there; just don't lose the picture," he added with a grin.

Losing the picture was a phrase used by experienced controllers when a green controller forgets momentarily the instructions he gave aircraft in his charge, which could lead to disastrous consequences. Johnny loved to play around and joke in the tower, but he was all business when it came to controlling aircraft.

The post housing list held a ninety to a hundred-twenty day wait, so Marie and I rented an old craftsman-style house in a quiet neighborhood in Enterprise, about three miles from the west gate of Rucker. Situated along a tree-lined street, the pale rose-colored asbestos sided house would be our new home. It was a two bedroom house with a gas fireplace in the living room, with French doors closing off the dining room, adding to the charm and romance of the old house. The bedrooms were nice sized, plenty of room for the girls to grow and play. A double carport gave plenty of room for the Cutlass and the Brown Bomber. It was perfect.

Days turned into weeks at Highbluff. I'd become certified in the tower in minimal time, and had earned back my Staff Sergeant stripes. The tower was a small, orange and white checkered tactical cab resting atop a twenty-foot trestle, facing perpendicular to eight paved landing strips. Two local controllers worked in harmony, with one working the four south lanes, and the other controller working the four on the north side, closest to the tower.

Air traffic flew in two concentric patterns to their assigned landing strips. Lanes one through four on the north side, and lanes five through eight on the south side. One wrong move would result in a tragic mid-air mistake. Constant verbal communication between controllers was imperative.

After a few months, I developed a severe case of hives working the steady stage field traffic. It was either an allergic reaction to the constant peanut pollen in the air, or the day after day rhythmic foot-tapping with a mike in one hand and a cigarette in the other. I kept this constant rhythm to time how long it took a UH-1 Huey to travel from one point in the traffic pattern to the next. After clearing one aircraft to land, I'd tap my knuckles on the console, move his flight strip, then clear the next one for takeoff. The hives got worse, spreading along both arms and covering my torso with red splotches. I'd go home at night, and Marie would casually ask me how my day went.

"What do you mean by that?" I'd snap.

We both decided that no job was worth all that, so I made an appointment with the flight surgeon. A thorough examination revealed a bad case of urticaria, a skin irritation caused by un unknown allergen, or by psychological stimuli. Appointments were set up for me to be evaluated at Keesler Air Force Base in Biloxi, and Eglin Air Force Base near Valparaiso, Florida. After being subjected to over a hundred allergy tests, and given several pills and salves to relieve the painful itching, my condition didn't improve, it just got worse.

When I returned to the flight surgeon's office to review the results of all the allergy tests, I was presented with an unwanted ultimatum. The flight surgeon was a soft-spoken Lieutenant Colonel, a bit on the portly die. Family pictures, awards, and diplomas adorned the walls of his office.

"Sergeant Smith," LTC Smith (no relation) began, "unfortunately, none of the tests showed anything for the cause of the problem other than stress."

"Now, where do we go with this, sir?"

"I have a suggestion. You may not like it, though. Apply for a medical discharge; there may be some VA compensation in it for you."

"Sorry, sir, that's out of the question. I don't want to get out. Isn't there another way?"

"Well," he pondered, "You could look for another job. I know ATC can be pretty stressful. Tell you what, take this number, call Master Sergeant Donahue at the ATC School, and ask him about a lateral transfer to become an instructor. You might like it. Oh, and hey, tell Pat to get a real job…we go back a ways."

I called MSG Patrick Donahue at the ATC School to set up an appointment for an interview, and filled Johnny in on the plan when I got back to Highbluff. He didn't like the idea of losing a controller, he understood something had to be done.

MSG Donahue talked at length about my coming on board as an instructor, and the procedure for transferring from USACC to the school. I mentioned that LTC Smith said to say hello, but to avoid seeming overly familiar, I though it best to forego passing along the message of friendly abuse.

After three weeks of instructor training, I joined the staff to teach non-radar procedures, the part of the school most feared by students, back on Tank Hill. That was a critical washout point. If a student didn't make it there, he or she was gone. Reclassified into another MOS.

I was being constantly subjected to new instructor initiation rituals by the closely-knit society of instructors in the non-radar section. Many of the NCOs and retirees serving as instructors shared a close bond. I was as welcome into the fold as any other NCO, but the experts were going to have their way with me. All part of the calculated plan to see how much I could endure, endless streams of flight strips kept piling up, one after another in the lab simulator. Three instructors acting as pilots calling inbound for non-radar separation instructions, called relentlessly over my headset.

The scenario called for up to fifteen aircraft to be separated vertically and longitudinally, then brought in for a safe landing following a radar failure at Approach Control. Relying on memory recall of spoken aircraft identifications, and location within the control zone, I had to respond to multiple calls while moving flight strips on the board and pass all aircraft over to the tower safely with minimal error. By the time the exercise was over, my score was a negative twelve. Sweating and shaking, I knew I had failed miserably.

Laughter erupted from the back of the lab. I turned around in my chair to see all the instructors from non-radar: fifteen or so military and civilian employees standing in a semi circle around the back of the lab laughing and hollering, "Gotcha!"

MSG Donahue, a stout , balding man in his early forties, walked over to me, slapped me on the back. "Congratulations, Smitty," he yelled over the crowd. "Consider yourself certified!"

Confused and embarrassed by the hour-long debacle, however elated the ordeal was over, I rose from my chair to accept handshakes and back slaps from the other instructors. I had become part of the brotherhood.

A few months later, an opening for a tower instructor at Kelly Hall was advertised. MSG Donahue called me into his office to see if I'd be interested in a transfer. "Basically, I need to have everyone crossed trained in all sections of the school," he said. "We have to move folks around a lot to fill in where they're needed. You can start up there next week. Just let me know ASAP if you'd like to do it now or later."

"Great! I'll be up there Monday," I said, trying to conceal my excitement.

Marie and I had been looking at houses in earnest for several weeks in hopes of owning our own home again. Our rented house in Enterprise was nice enough, but it wasn't ours. Much-needed renovations were necessary to update the old house, but the landlord never would have approved them.

An unassuming three bedroom brick ranch style house in Newton sort of spoke to us one Saturday afternoon in November '80. Newton was a sleepy little town about ten miles east of Daleville, a thriving Army town just outside Rucker's south gate. The ranch house in Newton was a real fixer, a bank repossession. Marie had studied art design at the University of Northern Iowa, and foresaw great possibilities for the old house

"It's got good bones," she said, envisioning what a few inexpensive cosmetic changes could make.

The house was not exactly a steal, but well within our budget. Loan approved and contract signed, we took possession of the house and immediately went to work transforming it into our home. The previous owners unmistakably were cat lovers. The entire house wreaked of cat urine and feces. It was everywhere in the house: in all the carpets, baseboards, closets, and even the kitchen cabinets. The furry little guys must have been climbers. All the carpets, padding, and some of the woodwork I couldn't clean, were ripped out and tossed in a pile in the yard. Beneath the carpet in each room, real hardwood floors waited to be sanded and rejuvenated.

One at a time, each room in the house was recarpeted, or the wood floors sanded and refinished. Slowly, the neglected house was turning into a warm, inviting home. As soon as our budget allowed it, the single carport was walled in, making the space more usable as a family room. Dark wood paneling, so popular in the seventies, was installed to give the new room a homey, comfortable look. A free-standing cone fireplace adorned the corner of the room. We'd made our mark on the old house, and sat back enjoying all the hard work that went into the transformation.

December, 1984, a family tragedy took us back to Iowa. My mother had suffered from breast cancer for several years, but always kept her pain from us. She didn't want us to worry about her. On Christmas Eve, my four sisters and my brother were at her bedside.

"I'm sorry I spoiled everyone's Christmas," Mom said weakly. Just like her, always putting others' feelings ahead of her own.

"Mom, you didn't spoil anyone's Christmas," I responded with tears rolling down my cheeks. "We all got together for Christmas. Remember the last time that ever happened?"

Later that evening, Mom passed away peacefully. That was the only time I saw Dad weep openly. They had shared a life together for more than fifty years, raising six kids through thick and thin, good and bad times. For years to come, Christmas held a far different meaning for me than it did when I was growing up.

Mid-May, 1985, Marie called me at work one morning to voice an opinion. Sometimes, I hated when she did that. It usually meant a big change of some kind.

"Don't you ever get tired of watching the same cars driving up and down the same street day after day?" I could see the point coming. "I sure do. Have you ever thought about going overseas again? I'd like to go to Hawaii, Alaska, or Japan. Doesn't really matter where. I just want to get out of Newton. I want to go to other places and see new things. Could you see about filling out a dream sheet before you come home tonight?"

"Uh, well," I stammered, trying to let her dissatisfaction soak in for a bit, "yeah, I could do that. What about the house?"

"I figured we could rent it out while we're gone…turn it over to a realtor, or something."

"Just like that?"

"Just like that."

"Okay, I'll see what I can do, but remember what happened the last time I tried for Hawaii?"

"That guy was an idiot. It's got to be different, now. There should be more slots available."

"Alright, I'll talk to personnel and try to call DA. Gotta go. Love you, see you tonight."

Right after I got off the phone with Marie, I ran into the school office to talk with my supervisor, Master Sergeant George Milano. George reminded me a lot of Johnny Edison. A quick wit, a player and a joker, but all business when it counted. I told him I'd like to call DA to see where the slots were, then run over to personnel to fill out the paperwork.

"Don't bother calling DA, I just got a new list from Ft Huachuca (headquarters for Army Air traffic Control, in Arizona). Plenty of slots. Pick a spot. You want overseas or CONUS?" (an acronym for Continental United States)

"Overseas, if I could get it."

"Go see SSG Wells at personnel. She'll hook you up. Here, take this 4187, fill it out real quick and take it over to her. Good luck. Hate to see you leave, though"

"Thanks, I just need to broaden my horizons," I called back as I strolled out the door.

Less than thirty days later, I had a set of orders for Germany. Germany? If I'd put in for Germany, I'd probably gotten Hawaii. That's military logic. Germany it was.

Marie and I did a lot of research on Germany and the rest of Europe over the next few weeks. We watched the mark rate slowly lose ground. In July, the rate was three marks to the dollar. My reporting date was 30 November, so we had plenty of time to pack, throw away stuff we moved around, but never used, and make plans for what we'd do in our spare time over there. Travel, skiing, learn the language. There were plenty of opportunities.

There was one thing I hadn't given a whole lot of thought to, though: Air traffic control units in Germany spent a lot of time in the field, so I needed to learn all I could about tactical ATC. The only contact I'd had with that was at the 'Wolf Pit' when I was a student in the school. We were graded on a two-day field exercise about twenty miles from post, using all the tactical equipment and procedures we'd read about, while controlling live aircraft. NCOs were expected to know those procedures used in the field, so I began burning the midnight oil again.

The moving company pulled up in front of the house almost to the day they said they would. Slowly and carefully, the container-laden flatbed was backed down the narrow driveway. Four men dismounted from the truck, and began the task of packing out our house with very little wasted motion. They were finished and had me signing shipping documents within three hours. Even if I wanted to, there was no turning back now.

Once more, the out processing job was done, and we were headed for a new life, far from home. The four of us were excited about the trip, however, Allison and Sarah only thought Daddy wore funny clothes to work, not even thinking that I was in the Army. They just knew we were moving, and that was a novelty for them. Living in a foreign land would be a whole new adventure for us all.

13. Germany, Time to Mature

The 747 US Air Atlantic Clipper continued steadily on its assigned course through the predawn darkness. Stars trembled above, as somewhere beneath the carpet of wispy clouds sprawled the dark waters of the Atlantic.

The dim, cramped cabin was hushed, except for the restless snoring of countless GI's, and the murmuring of young mothers trying to comfort babies long since bored with the seemingly endless flight from Charleston. No small wonder people called these nightly MAC flights to Germany 'cattle cars'. It was not unlike riding in the back seat of a Toyota for seven hours. And, there wasn't really a whole lot to do to while the hours away.

If a guy felt like listening to music over the seat radio, or watch a movie, he could procure some of those hermetically sealed plastic earphones from the flight attendant to enjoy a first run flick like *Gremlins*, or *Cocoon*. After Marie and I watched both movies, while Allison and Sarah played and dozed, we all closed our eyes and tried to get some rest. I'd read all the magazines I'd cared to, and sat watching Marie and the girls trying to enjoy a few minutes of blissful sleep among that sea of restless, weary humanity.

Soldiers of all ranks and experiences were aboard US Air Flight 31 to Frankfurt that night. Looking around, musing at the possibilities my new assignment would offer, I knew my first task would be to become certified in the control tower. After spending the last five years teaching control tower procedures at Kelly hall, this would be a new and exciting challenge. With various ATC procedures and phraseology running through my mind like an ear worm, at last I gave into a fitful sleep.

Feeling the weightlessness of descent and the decreasing hum of the Jumbo jet's engines being throttled back, I roused up to see Marie and the girls still sleeping. The first rays of morning sun steamed through the windows, filling the cabin with a golden glow.

"Good morning, ladies and gentlemen," came the Captain's voice over the intercom from the flight deck. "We're beginning our descent into Rhein-Main Air Force Base. The weather in Frankfurt is a balmy 27 degrees Fahrenheit with light scattered clouds. We'll be touching down in about twelve minutes. Hope you all had a pleasant flight, and behalf of the crew and myself, I'd like to thank you for flying US Airways. Welcome to Germany, and enjoy your stay."

The sudden roar of the heavy jet's engines being reversed and the pull of the brakes slowing the plane down on the runway brought Marie and the girls out of their slumber.

"We're here!" Allison called out sleepily, rubbing her eyes and yawning.

"Oh boy!" Sarah added.

"Yes we are," Marie reassured them. "Now don't get up until the pilot stops the plane, then you can put your backpacks on and get ready, okay?"

Once the pilot taxied to a stop at the terminal, a covered gangway was rolled out to dock with the plane. Weary passengers stood up stretching kinks out after the overnight flight, retrieving luggage from the overhead bins, and waited patiently for their turns to deplane. Slowly, the line began to move toward the international customs gate.

The lobby on the far side of the customs terminal was swarming with greeters of the new arrivals from Charleston. Soldiers in uniform, and families stood with anxious anticipation, watching for friends and family to emerge from the long hallway. Signs depicting the last names of new arrivals identified the sponsors of incoming soldiers.

Locating my name emblazoned on a small poster being held up by a young soldier wearing buck sergeant stripes, I edged through the waiting throng with Marie and the girls in tow.

"You must be Kurt," I said, extending a handshake greeting.

"Sergeant Smith, welcome to Germany. I'm Kurt Messina, and this is Jimmy Hyatt."

"Pleasure, guys, thanks for picking us up." Kurt was assigned by the unit in Ansbach as my sponsor. We'd talked several times on the phone before I started out-processing at Rucker. He'd sent me unit packets telling of housing possibilities in the Ansbach area. During those phone conversations, Kurt had warned me about a power hungry E6 who would more than likely try to compete with me for the Facility Chief's job when I became certified. His unrelenting question to Kurt was, "What's this guy's rank and time in grade?" Kurt would always reply that mine was far and above his. Actually, I had about eight months on him. Kurt was relieved to learn that he may not have to work for Staff Sergeant Kevin Haynes, a tyrannical ex-MP with very few people skills.

Kurt was a stract young troop, standing tall in his starched fatigues and spit-shined jump boots. He had an air of self assurance coupled with a bit of arrogance about him. Jimmy, on the other hand, stood just under six feet, looking a bit overweight. His wrinkled uniform and scuffed boots indicated more of a flare for doing his job as a controller than looking like the soldier of the month.

"Thanks again, guys. This is my wife Marie, and Allison and Sarah. Say hi to the nice men, girls."

"Hi Mr. Kurt, hi Mr. Jimmy," Allison said with instilled courtesy.

"Hi Mr. Kurt, hi Mr. Jimmy," Sarah parroted respectfully.

Pleased and amused with our daughters' cherubic politeness, Kurt and Jimmy led us to the baggage claim area, then on to their Army van waiting in the parking lot.

The drive south to Ansbach was a nearly two hour journey through storybook scenery along the Autobahn. Early morning mists shrouded snow covered forests and hills. Picturesque villages made up of centuries-old architecture adorned the countryside. Germany had revealed the romantic draw we'd anticipated.

Audis, Mercedes, BMWs, and other exotic European cars roared past on the three lane superhighway. No speed limits were posted for the open Autobahn. The olive drab green Volkswagen van hummed along at a respectable sixty miles per hour, with no thoughts of competing with its supercar counterparts.

The conversation inside the van ranged from Kurt's constant haranguing dialogue about the woes of the unit in Ansbach to the dictatorship of SSG Haynes. He even added that he and Jimmy had driven up to Frankfurt the night before, and proceeded to get hammered barhopping, and barely making it to Rhein- Main on time to pick us up.

Recalling past experiences with arriving at new assignments, meeting new friends, and occasionally catching Marie's disapproving glances during Kurt's observations, I decided the best course of action was to feign sleep for the rest of the trip. Over the years, Marie and I had become pros at making our own judgments about people and places, vowing not to be led astray or disillusioned by chronic complainers and nay sayers.

Ansbach was a beautiful old city nestled in a tree-rimmed valley in Southern Bavaria. Another ancient city steeped in rich Gothic architecture. Rebuilt after being partially destroyed by allied bombings during World

War II, the bustling city of nearly 70,000 was a center of commerce and agriculture. Surrounded by fertile farmland interlaced with dense forests, this would be our home for the next three years.

Kurt drove through town to the airfield at Katterbach, a small farming community about six kilometers north of Ansbach. Formerly a strategically important Luftwaffe Air base during the war, the airfield was now the home of the 1st Armored Division, 114th Aviation Brigade. Hueys, Blackhawks, OH-58's, and Cobra gunships were parked side by side in endless rows on the grassy airfield. Later plans for paving up to fifty two acres of parking ramp were in the works.

A row of old Luftwaffe barracks stood in silent sentinel along the main street running through the kaserne to the aviation brigade headquarters. The control tower was thirty foot extension of the three story building, centered on the structure, overlooking the airfield.

Pulling up in front of Brigade Headquarters, Kurt invited me to follow him to the orderly room on the third floor of the proud old building. Marie and the girls stayed behind in the van, retrieving books and small toys from their backpacks to keep them occupied until I returned.

After signing into 3rd Platoon, Charlie Company, 58th Aviation Battalion with instructions to report to Schwabisch Hall, the battalion headquarters, first thing in the morning for an in-briefing, Kurt ran us over to the guest house about a mile and a half away. On the way, Marie asked Kurt to point out the dispensary for her. The kids had a history of getting hurt somehow while Daddy was at work, and Mom was always saddled with the task of taking them to be healed. Kurt doubled back and pulled around to the front door of the clinic, which was conveniently behind the tower, noting that it was open twenty-four hours.

That night, we were all sound asleep in our European feather beds when a blood-curdling scream came from the other bedroom where the girls were sleeping. Marie and I both jumped out of bed, rushed into the other room to find that Allison had fallen out of bed and bloodied her nose on the edge of the coffee table. More scared than hurt, she was cleaned up and comforted, and back sound asleep in a few minutes.

The old mechanical alarm clock on the hotel night stand jerked me awake at 0500 with an obnoxious clanging. Quick shower and shave, dressed in pressed fatigues and shined boots, I was ready for the day. Grabbing a pop tart and my briefcase, I kissed Marie goodbye and headed out the door. Kurt was waiting in the cold predawn in the VW van. We headed down the road toward the gate, then turned right towards Ansbach.

Early morning traffic was beginning to pick up, with soldiers reporting for duty, and Germans going to work.

Schwabisch Hall was situated several miles off the Autobahn. A winding drive through the mountains and foothills took us through some of the most breathtaking scenery I'd seen in the twenty-four hours we'd been in Germany. Finally at our destination, Kurt wheeled up in front of Battalion Headquarters.

"Here we are," he pointed out. "I'm headed over to the PX, but I'll be back in a couple of hours to see how you're doing. Go right through those double doors and see the First Sergeant. Have fun."

Processing in to the battalion didn't take near as long as Kurt figured, so after I was done with everything, I had time to chat with a few familiar folks I'd known from Rucker. I recognized Master Sergeant Janet Coleman, from Base Field Branch at Rucker, as my new First Sergeant. I first met her when I came back to Rucker after my short break in service.

"Good to see you again, Top," I said. "Playing any ball this year?" 1SG Coleman was the coach of the women's post softball league back at Rucker.

"I don't think so, too much going on here. You bring your family?"

"Yes, they're at the guest house in Katterbach."

"Trip okay? I know it's a long flight."

"Oh, it wasn't too bad. It was a bit long, but I was glad to get off that plane."

"Well, you ready to go to work? I've got you as Training NCO, and after you get rated, you'll be Mike Elia's tower chief. He's ATC chief at Katterbach."

"What about Haynes? Isn't he in line for that job?"

"Don't worry about him. He's GCA. He thinks he's going to the tower, but I have other plans for him."

"Let me ask you something, off the record," she continued, "what sort of shape was SGT Messina in when he picked you up in Frankfurt?"

"Well," I said, feeling a little on the spot with that question, "he seemed a bit under the weather, and kept complaining about the way Haynes treated people, and how bad things were in the platoon."

"Had he been drinking?" Red flags were going up. Be careful, Smith, I cautioned myself.

"I don't believe so. I didn't notice anything. Why?"

"Messina has a history of alcohol abuse."

"He did mention he was in Frankfurt the night before, but he didn't indicate that he'd gone out or anything."

"Just be on the lookout. Let me know if anything comes up. He's on my list."

"Roger that." I felt that being put in that position was not a good sign.

Most of the trip back to Katterbach was quiet and uneventful. Kurt didn't talk a whole lot. Finally, I broke the ice. "Hey, what's between you and Haynes?" I began, hoping for some answers.

"Why?" he sounded guarded.

"Just wondering. I asked Coleman, she said he's GCA and won't be going to the tower."

"He's got a nasty habit of spying on people and stickin' his nose where it don't belong, then runnin' to Battalion with it. That's how he gets his rocks off. Like he's some kinda hero."

"Has he ever spied on you?"

"Who knows. It's a small place."

"Have you ever drank on the job or showed up for work hung over?"

"Where's this goin', Sergeant Smith?" he was becoming defensive, so I backed off.

"Hey, Sarge, chill. I'm just trying to get the facts straight so I know how to deal with Haynes, that's all." Trying to defuse the situation now would prevent it from being blown out of proportion later.

I couldn't help wondering about Kurt Messina, though. I did detect a faint odor of beer when he and Jimmy picked us up in Frankfurt. I also began to wonder what everyone's motivation was for all the back-stabbing I'd been hearing about. The burning questions were: Why did the First Sergeant want me to rat out someone that I just met and knew very little about? And what did Kurt Messina have to hide? Why did he get so defensive?

The winter sun was beginning to set, adding more chill to the air as we pulled into the guest house parking lot. Thanking Kurt for driving me to Schwabisch hall, I entered through the hallway door, hearing the chatter of children in the various rooms. Opening the door to our room, I was greeted jubilantly by two little Smith girls. "Daddy's home!" they both yelled at the same time.

"What happened to you, Sweetie? I asked, turning to Allison, looking at her face. Both eyes were darkened by bruising, and she was sporting a pretty nasty goose egg on her forehead.

"I fell out of bed last night, Daddy, remember? Doctor says I'll be okay in a few days, though."

I looked wide-eyed at Marie, she returned my gaze with a nod and that crooked little smile she gives me whenever an almost expected childhood disaster occurs.

"It's a good thing Kurt showed us where the dispensary was. This place doesn't even have an ice machine to make a cold pack, so I bundled them both up and hiked the mile and a half to see the doctor."

"Wow! Is her nose broken?" I asked, trying not to seem as alarmed as I actually was. I hated seeing my babies hurt.

"You okay, Sweetie?" I consoled Allison, gently touching the surgical tape across her swollen nose.

"Ow! Daddy, it hurts!" she protested.

"Gee, I wonder how many trips we'll have to make over there until they start calling you kids by your first names, you know, like they did at Rucker?" I pondered, rubbing my chin, trying to relieve the tension with a little humor, but no one was laughing. Except Sarah. She found humor in just about everything.

Supper, baths, and then into bed. With the girls tucked in for the night, and their bedroom furniture rearranged to prevent any more nighttime catastrophes, Marie and I laid down to share discussions about our separate days.

The waiting list for family housing was nine months to a year, so once again, the apartment search was underway. With the help of new friends in the platoon, we located and were moved into a newly finished apartment in Rugland, a small farming community about fourteen kilometers from the airfield. It was a nicely furnished loft on the third floor of a house. Beautifully finished in pine paneling on the ceilings, skylights allowed light to stream into the living room and bathroom. Plastered walls accented the ceramic tile floors. The girls each had their own bedroom, which at their preteen ages was almost a necessity. Each room was adequately sized, enough room for all of our furniture on its way from Alabama.

Nine months had passed, and the mark rate had dropped to two marks thirty-five to the dollar. No longer being able to afford to live in Rugland, we signed for leased housing in Oberichenbach, just across the road from the airfield. We would miss the scenic vista from our third floor apartment, as well as the isolation and tranquility of living off-post. The townhouse apartment in Oberichenbach was very attractive, however. The other occupants of our housing area were all senior NCOs. Each apartment actually had four levels including an unfinished attic with a concrete floor. Such things were unheard of back in the states. I placed an area rug and some toys in the attic so the girls could have some extra play space.

While living in Rugland, I studied my facility training manual every night until the wee hours of the morning, learning the layout of the airfield, memorizing radio frequencies, and procedures governing the operations of the ATC control zone. It was a little strange converting distance from miles to kilometers, feet to meters, and millibars to the European heptopescales. Everything was metric. It took some getting used to. I was rated in the Katterbach tower in record time, ready to take on the awesome task of Tower Chief.

The following months were rigorous, to say the least. Battalion field exercises came almost once a month, preluded by an early morning phone call, alerting us to be on station in thirty minutes or less. After convoying to an appointed location, the portable tactical tower and GCA radar was set up and tested. Remote navigational aids were installed to complete the tactical airfield. The installation of all the ATC equipment was closely monitored by battalion evaluators. Always snooping out problem areas, they were called 'battalion weasels.'

16 May, 1986, on a dark, rainy morning, a company alert was called. "Whiz quiz," came the voice of the CQ, "formation in thirty minutes."

I looked at the clock---0400. I jumped out of bed, dressed, laced up my boots, and ran out the door to the car. These battalion urinalyses were few and far between, but usually took a disastrous toll. Someone was always caught hot with either alcohol or drugs in their system. This morning's test was no different, but the casualty rate was unexpectedly high. Master Sergeant Danny Morris, our easy-going platoon sergeant, who loved to drink German beer off duty, and Kurt Messina, both tested positive for alcohol. I had my own conspiracy theory about this morning's pop quiz, but I kept my thoughts to myself.

Mike Elia, whom I've never trusted since he accused me several months ago of watching his apartment, counting the racks of German beer he took from his car into the house. Trying to explain to him that after spending every weekend sitting and drinking with him and his wife wasn't setting a very good example for my kids. However, he took it as a personal insult that I quit drinking at his house every weekend.

One Sunday afternoon as we were leaving to go home, Allison asked innocently, "Daddy, are you drunk again? Is that why Mommy's driving?" That was the end of that. No more sitting and drinking . We had Europe at our feet. Traveling would be the new entertainment. Ancient cities, castles, beautiful scenery. We'd do it all, enjoying the culture and customs of Germany and beyond.

The other side of the theory was that Elia and Coleman were old friends, and after doing a little research on my own, I discovered that they both disliked Danny Morris and went to great lengths to help him foul his own career.

Following that debacle, I kept pretty much to myself, enjoying traveling with my family, and working hard at my jobs as tower chief and training NCO. It was at that time I decided to begin chronicling my experiences with people and places in Germany. Additionally, there was always constant drama going on within the platoon and its members in Ansbach, the driving rationale was, "I could write a book about this place." Evolutionary thoughts began to develop, encompassing life experiences as a soldier, husband, and father into perspective. A book of memoirs could quite possibly be the culmination of this literary pursuit.

My assignment in Germany was not all tension and hardship. It had its lighter moments. Our battalion was involved in a REFORGER (Return of Forces to Germany) near Wurzburg in the early spring of 1986. Our task would be to set up a remote ATC site on a mountaintop. An AN/TRN-30 non-directional radio beacon had to be installed and flight-checked before the end of the afternoon. Murphy's Law dictated that whatever could get screwed up, did.

The beacon was installed according to the manual, but we had no luck getting it to work. The most ideal location for it was in the middle of a clearing along a tree-lined ridge. Not having enough clearance for one of the hundred-foot guy wires, it was secured to a tree trunk at the edge of the clearing. After erecting the 60 foot mast atop the beacon canister, we tested for a signal. The faint dot-dash-dot Morse Code beeping told us it was up and running, but with an unsatisfactorily weak signal.

"Army 421, Wolf Pack 58, radio check, over," I called over the PRC-77 to the battalion U-21 orbiting the mountain waiting to flight check the radio beacon.

"Wolf Pack 58, Army 421, loud and clear, standing by for flight check, over," Captain Lawson, Headquarters Company CO, and the pilot of the battalion flight check bird, replied.

"Roger, Army 421, report beacon inbound"

"421 outbound now, see you in a few."

The gray Beechcraft King Air made a wide right turn off in the distance, beginning his approach from the south back toward the ridge to check the signal on the radio beacon. A successful flight check of the beacon would mean a welcomed end to a long day and some evening chow followed by some much needed rest.

The U-21 roared overhead, banking sharply to the east away from the ridge, with no beacon report. Something wasn't right.

"Wolf Pack 58, 421, no joy on the beacon," came the disappointing report from CPT Lawson.

"Army 421, roger, will advise," I replied.

"Get C and E up here to check this thing out!" I yelled to Jimmy Hyatt. "Everyone else start checking these guy lines!"

Minutes later, Sergeant Steve Benson from C and E came sliding up in a green camouflaged Blazer to check out the disabled radio beacon. I was glad someone else knew more about tactical ATC equipment than I did. Being less of an expert, I learned to rely heavily on the expertise of young controllers and the guys from C and E.

SGT Benson ran a series of quick diagnostic checks on the beacon, but after several minutes of dead ends, he was ready to give up. Jimmy Hyatt, one of the best tactical controllers in Charlie Company, had a gift for solving problems not many others could. While we were all standing around analyzing the problem and considering the consequences of an overall poor performance on a battalion exercise during REFORGER, Jimmy had been snooping around the four foot tall beacon canister.

"Hey guys, come over here and look at this! You're not gonna believe this!" he shouted.

We all hightailed it over to where Jimmy was squatting next to the antenna coupling assembly (commonly known as the 'trash can'), pointing to a blown fuse on the beacon radio transmitter. Wasting no time or motion, Benson grabbed a fuse from his tool kit, replacing the rogue fuse, then motioned for Jimmy to crank up the 1.5 KW generator. He flipped the beacon power switch back on. Success! A strong Morse Code signal finally emitted from the transmitter.

"Get Captain America (Benson's pet name for CPT Lawson) back on the horn and have him make another pass. We'll get this sucker done, yet," he promised.

We held our collective breath as CPT Lawson banked into a wide left turn, heading back inbound to the beacon.

"Wolf Pack 58, 421, beacon inbound, loud and strong. Good job, guys. 421 out."

We all jumped and shouted, doing the chest bump like a bunch of NFL players after a game-winning touchdown. Jimmy received his share of back slaps and head noogies for saving the day.

It wasn't all good, though. In the end, we'd succeeded in passing the radio beacon installation and operational test. But earlier in the day, Major Maddox, a hard-bitten ex-infantryman, and our battalion XO (executive officer), arrived for a surprise inspection of the beacon site. Right away, I could tell he wasn't very happy about the beacon not being up to par. His normal smiling face was replaced with a scowl.

"Sergeant Smith," he began in a low voice, "What the hell is going on here? Why isn't this beacon operational yet?"

Not trying to sound defeated, I replied, "It's got a weak signal, but we're working on it, sir."

Expecting the worst from the XO, I kept my team checking and rechecking the entire system, hoping against hope it would suddenly come to life while he was still in the area, but no luck. An intermittent, diluted signal was all the beacon could muster.

"Come over here, Sergeant Smith," MAJ Maddox commanded, standing next to the beacon canister. "All you NCOs get over here, too." Jimmy was just a Spec 4, but he sidled over to join the group standing in a semi-circle with the XO standing next to the beacon.

"I want everyone to take their right hand," MAJ Maddox exclaimed, holding up his right hand to demonstrate, "and place it on top of this damned beacon." Looking helplessly at each other, I thought, "What the hell is this guy up to?"

"Now, take off your hats and bow your heads." With our right hands on the beacon, we did as the XO directed. By that time, everyone had the realization that MAJ Maddox's warped sense of humor was calculated to help us all make the best of a bad situation. He wanted us to silently pray over the stubborn radio beacon.

Later that night, we all sat around in the cadre tent, laughing and joking about the day's fiasco. Jimmy got up, stretched, picked up his flashlight, heading out to the latrine. Not quite the comforts of home, the German port-a-pot served us much better than the dark side of a tree. A few minutes later, he came tearing breathlessly back into the tent, with a look of terror on his face.

"There...there's some kind of damned German night creature out there!" he stammered. "It's inside the port-a-john!" Grabbing his Louieville Slugger from underneath his bunk, Jimmy headed back out the door toward the outhouse with the rest of us at his heals, laughing and teasing the poor guy along the way.

Gingerly, Jimmy opened the outhouse door with the business end of the bat. Out of the darkness of the portable toilet, a squirrel ran up the bat, did a three-sixty around the terrified Jimmy's head and shoulders, scampering off into the woods. I hadn't laughed that hard in a long time. The incident with Jimmy's German night creature was a definite takeoff on Ray Stevens' comedic *The Day the Squirrel Went Berserk.*

Back at Katterbach, poor Jimmy continued to battle his weight problem. Overweight since high school, he'd gone to extreme lengths to avoid being chaptered out of the Army. Someone suggested he try Ex Lax, guaranteeing a rapid weight loss. Poor guy ended up in the emergency room with an IV in his arm, on the verge of dehydration. Later, Jimmy sought help through diet pills from the flight surgeon. When he went to the pharmacy to pick up his prescription, he was mistakenly given some strong tranquilizers meant for someone else. I found him in the mess hall an hour later, face down in his mashed potatoes, sound asleep. If it weren't for bad luck, poor Jimmy wouldn't have any luck at all.

My three years in Germany were a mixture of fun, laughter, travel, and unforgettable career experiences. However, personal tragedies also played a major role in the maturation process. Early one Friday morning around 0630, I received a phone call from my older sister, Bette.

"Dad passed away last night," she began tearfully. "He's just been going downhill since Mom died. His will to live was just gone."

Choking back the tears, I responded, "I'll be home as soon as I can get a flight."

It would take most of the day to coordinate with the Red Cross, and driving to Schwabisch Hall to have an emergency leave form signed by the battalion commander. Thankfully, when I arrived in the orderly room at the airfield to fill out a leave form, MAJ Maddox was there on company business.

"I'm sorry for your loss," he offered. "Maybe this will make things a little brighter." He presented me with a copy of promotion orders for Sergeant First Class, another rung in the career ladder I'd been anticipating for almost eight years.

After an impromptu promotion ceremony, the XO added with compassion and dignity, "Let me sign those leave papers for you. Save you a trip to the Hall."

Thanking MAJ Maddox and everyone in the orderly room that morning for their kindness and support, while trying to remain composed and professional in light of flying home to bury my father, I left to return home and pack for the trip back across the Atlantic.

The entire flight to Iowa, I mulled over in my mind the life lessons Dad had taught me. How to give and get respect, to make good choices, and ultimately, how to be a father.

After Mom was taken from us on Christmas Eve, 1984, with cancer, Dad was lost without her. He spent the twilight of his life in the Iowa Veterans' Home in Marshalltown, in ever-declining health. He'd say, "I just want to go be with Mom."

Following the funeral, complete with military honors rendered by the American Legion Post in Marshalltown, of which Dad had been Past Commander, I learned that my brother Dennis, fifteen months my senior, was terminally ill and was given less than two years to live. He suffered from ARC (AIDS-Related Complex), which had devastated his immune system. Dennis had chosen a lifestyle of drug and alcohol abuse, and gay relationships since high school. He would pay a heavy and lasting toll. Never agreeing with his choices, I always loved and accepted him. He was still my brother.

Returning to Germany, all feelings of loss, anger, and denial of losing Dad, then learning of Dennis' impending death, boiled to the surface. Marie met me in the parking lot of our apartment building to find me on my knees weeping. I could no longer hold back the cleansing flood of tears. In that respect, I was much like my father, I rarely allowed my emotions to show.

The following months until my tour was up, field exercises were preceded by early morning alert phone calls. During my off time, Marie and I would pack up the car and kids, heading for parts unknown, taking every opportunity to travel across Europe that our budget would allow.

Finally, the end of our three years in Germany had arrived, and the out-processing would begin again. I was being reassigned to Ft Stewart, Georgia, home of the 24th Infantry Division. A sudden overnight snow storm had shattered our plans for a company van transporting my family and I to Frankfurt. Learning long ago to adapt, improvise, and overcome, I purchased train tickets from Ansbach to Frankfurt, with a stopover to change trains in Wurzburg. Once again, Marie and I and the kids set out on a journey of new beginnings, unencumbered by the fear of the unknown. We were an Army family.

To epitomize the black comedy of errors of the past three years, the main contributors, to the best of my knowledge, disappeared into the sunset in the following manners:

Kevin Haynes-- Got out of the Army after fourteen years due to being passed over for promotion to Sergeant First Class too many times.

Kurt Messina--Chaptered out of the Army for excessive alcohol-related offenses, returning to his old job as a male stripper at Chippendales in Las Vegas.

Danny Morris--His career still intact even after personal vendettas instigated by Elia and Coleman, he was reassigned to Hunter Army Airfield in Savannah, as First Sergeant.

Mike Elia--After three DUIs at Ft Rucker, and two in Germany, he was promoted to Master Sergeant and took a position on the battalion eval staff at Ft Bragg. Imagine that. Mike Elia a battalion weasel.

MAJ Maddox--Retired from the Army and entered the ministry.

Jimmy Hyatt--Chaptered out of the Army on the overweight program, then married a beautiful young Air Force nurse, and bought a house near Robbins Air Force Base, Georgia.

Steve Benson--Started a used car business in Baton Rouge, Louisiana.

14. A Soldier's Diary

Reporting in at Hunter Army Airfield in Savannah was like coming home. Danny Morris, my Platoon Sergeant in Germany, was the First Sergeant of 2nd Platoon, Alpha Company, 1/58 Aviation Regiment. Danny and I traveled to Ft Stewart, about fifty miles southwest of Savannah, to begin the ordeal of inprocessing. He stayed with me every step of the way, using his contacts there to ensure that I'd be assigned to Hunter. Wright Army Airfield served Ft Stewart, but it would be more advantageous for me to be assigned to 2nd Platoon at Hunter.

While earning my new certification at Hunter, I was also responsible for the tactical tower section located at our motor pool. Lessons learned, and experience and expertise gained under fire in Germany would be put to good use.

Marie didn't think very much of the post housing at Hunter. "Too dark and dingy, aside from being way too small." she commented. "Let's just leave them for junior enlisted families."

Determined to find comfortable and enjoyable living quarters for our family, Marie and Danny's wife Margaret perused the local paper for days, persevering in locating a nice apartment convenient to Hunter that would meet our needs: modern construction and plenty of room.

Hunter was far and away more complex than the airfield at Katterbach. With nearly a two mile long runway, it would accommodate heavy aircraft the likes of C-5s and B-52s. Additionally, L1011s and 747s would ferry troops to battle missions in foreign lands, often during the darkness of night. In December, 1989, several dozen C130 Hercules transports were launched at two minute intervals, carrying US Army Rangers of the 75th Ranger Regiment to participate in the invasion of Panama. Heavy commercial aircraft loaded with troops and equipment-laden military transports became an increasingly familiar sight landing and taking off from Hunter at all hours of the day and night.

6 August 1990, 0200 hours. Another phone call in the middle of the night. The Staff Duty NCO mechanically announced, "Victory Laser,

report in BDUs only." Okay, no problem. Probably be over by noon at the latest. Just another long day. Boy, was I wrong!

CPT Kelly Miranda, our CO, brought the platoon together around 1000 hrs to tell us what she knew. A situation in the Middle East was heating up, and quite possibly, 2nd Platoon, Alpha Company, would be a part of it.

Looking around the conference room to gather expressions from the CO's comments, I saw a mixture of fear, anxiety, and '*oh boys*' from those of the Rambo mentality. Young kids who joined the peace time Army who fancied themselves as a sort of super hero or gun-toting Commie-killer. Their ships finally came in. They would get their chances. Those of us who joined up during the Vietnam era secretly wished that we'd just be given the chance to preserve freedom and the American way.

The alert continued for several days, each more grueling than the last. Equipment was inventoried and packed in conexes, weapons were cleaned and checked, trucks and generators received preventive maintenance checks and services. Amazingly, all the parts that had been on back order for the trucks and generators, but hadn't been received for one reason or another, magically began arriving. Steadily, my deadline report grew slimmer by the day until nothing but a blank page remained.

Brand new equipment was ordered and received almost in the same day. Sergeant Taylor, the supply sergeant (magician) worked long, hard hours pulling strings, bartering, and angering her connections to get what we needed, and more. When all was said and done, we would be battle-ready, thanks to the *blank check* philosophy passed down from Brigade. After nearly two weeks, every piece of equipment, every truck, every roll of camouflage netting, and every tent peg was packed and loaded on board ships docked at the Georgia Ports Authority in Garden City.

With each passing day, the fervor of long-lost patriotism, killed during the Vietnam War, was returning to an emotional crescendo. American flags were proudly flown in front of homes and businesses, car antennas, or being carried down the streets by people displaying their praise and support of both soldiers being deployed to the Middle east, and President Bush's resolve not to back down from international terrorism.

Driving into post one day, I stopped at a traffic light on Eisenhower at Waters, looking at a car driving through the intersection with Old Glory flying proudly from its antenna. It struck me so hard and fast, I just sat behind the wheel and wept. Not because I was deploying to Saudi, but I realized that public support for this thing was everywhere, and patriotism had returned to the hearts of Americans.

Yellow and blue ribbons blossomed on trees, fences, and car antennas everywhere. Lee Greenwood's "Proud to be an American", which hadn't yet found its way into the dusty archives of country music, was returning even stronger as a patriotic icon. Certain Christmas carols and old, traditional hymns had the same effect on the soul as that song did.

When the day finally arrived that Alpha Company would deploy to Saudi, I came in the house and kissed Marie and the girls hello as always. However, when something's bothering one of us, a lingering kiss would be an indicator to find a quiet corner and talk. That afternoon, the kiss lingered. I looked at Marie, trying not to betray my emotions, and said, "I'm going to Saudi Arabia."

Marie gave me a strange, sideways glance, a sort of 'stop bullshitting me' look. The look in my eyes portrayed the reality. We held each other and wept. Old memories returned of indefinite separation, and quite possibly a painful and premature death in Vietnam. For us, fortunately, that fate never came to fruition.

We talked and held each other into the early morning hours. Marie and I always had an understanding about what life would be like without the other. If death was the cause of separation, the survivor would carry on life and raise the kids in the best way possible.

After countless delays, Alpha Company, 2nd Platoon was finally summoned to the gym at Hunter for primary lock-in. Rumors had it that a shakedown for contraband was to take place. As it turned out, there was no harassment, no shakedown. Final equipment checks were made, wills and financial matters were finalized, medical records were checked, and typhoid, cholera, and tetanus shots were administered.

Senior NCOs suggested everyone try and get a little sleep, so weary soldiers stretched out on the ground outside the gym to relax. Any sleep that night was replaced by murmured conversations of the eminent deployment. About three hours later, the order was passed through the darkness to board the bus for the short trip to one of the large hangars on the airfield, where we were integrated into a sea of restless humanity already there. The hangar was a holding point for troops and duffle bags before boarding the planes. Our last stop before the real trip, what has been anticipated, delayed, and for which so many goodbyes that were said the past few weeks, was at hand.

Families and friends were allowed visits to their soldier husbands and wives, coldly separated by a chain link fence around the perimeter of the airfield. The steel fence only prevented certain situations from occurring, however. One desperate couple was caught dead in the act of releasing their raging hormones under cover of darkness. Wow, right through the fence! That would seem a physically impossible human feat, but apparently that young soldier and his lady companion had it all down to a science.

Finally, a line of trucks pulled up to the hangar to load duffel bags and rucksacks, taking them to the waiting plane. More buses would appear to carry the next chalk to the DAGC point for their final briefing.

Once we dismounted the buses at the DAGC hangar, the white, unmarked 747 sat waiting to fly us off into the night. A miracle of timing in itself, it was the only thing that had been accomplished on schedule in the past three and a half weeks. Earlier in the evening, I called Marie to say that 0400 hours was our planned departure time. She promised she'd be there to watch the plane take off, knowing she could not see me, or say goodbye again.

The heavy 747 taxied slowly toward Runway 27 at Hunter Army Airfield. Things that were so familiar to me for the last year and a half or so, now seemed so distant. The tower, the fire station at its base, the GCA building and orderly room next to it, were no more than ghostly shells in the darkness, but each structure held a measure of importance to the flight operations at Hunter.

Catching a brief glimpse of the spectator bleachers, a small flashing light grabbed my attention. It was almost like a beacon in the night, sending out a Morse Code signal, *I love you and I'll miss you.* Next to the flashing light, someone was waving an American flag, a sight that would bring a tear to the eye of whoever saw it through the plane's window.

At 0430 hours, the unmarked, white 747 rumbled down the runway, climbing into the predawn darkness. Rushing past the tower and DAGC point, I saw the flashing light and flag waver once more. One last look at the tower brought thoughts of how many aircraft I'd cleared into and out of Hunter from that cab, and who would be working shift this morning.

Leveling off at a departure altitude of three thousand feet, the heavy jet was vectored on course by Savannah departure control. I closed my eyes, surrendering to light sleep. From time to time, I opened my eyes, out of restlessness, I supposed, and gazed out the window into the darkness. At one point, one of God's light shows was revealed at thirty thousand feet. Lightning flashed rhythmically, illuminating distant clouds from the inside. An awesome display, yet one with unfathomable energy.

0605 hours. The plane touched down at JFK in New York, for food service replenishing and refueling. At 0720, we were on our way to Rome, our next stop. How cool it would be to do a little sight-seeing, I thought. But that was a distinct impossibility right then.

1543 hours. We arrived in Rome, 2143 hours local time. An efficient Italian service crew hurried through the midship doors, performing their jobs with urgency and precision. After nearly an hour, we were in the air again. Next stop, Dhahran, Saudi Arabia.

The crew of flight attendants continually praised the soldiers on board for what we were doing, and how proud they were to serve us on the flight. The pilot reported over the intercom that he had a twenty year-old son, a truck driver in the Marines deployed to Saudi Arabia. He announced that his job with Tower Air was to shuttle troops to the Middle East, and that all those flights and the GIs aboard them had a special place in his heart, and that his and the entire crew's thoughts and prayers were with us.

Throughout the night on the flight to Dhahran, several bone-weary GIs dressed in desert camouflage uniforms stood in and around the two galleys of the 747, chatting with the flight attendants and doling out soft drinks and coffee to their counterparts, giving the crew a much-deserved break.

Sometime during the night on the flight from Rome to Dhahran, someone began presenting subdued rank insignias to each of the flight attendants to wear on their uniforms. Such collections spread like wildfire among the flight crew, and they began wearing every insignia from private to colonel. Next, Sharpies appeared so that their white uniform blouses could be covered in autographs.

As the white 747 glided to final approach altitude on Dhahran's TACAN (tactical air navigation system), the morning sun burst over the eastern horizon, casting first, an eerie purple-gray, then orange glow over the barren desert landscape. Oil pipelines, pumping stations, and cement factories broke up the endless sea of sand dunes.

Touching down and rolling out to the taxiway, we passed row after row of Marine Twin Cobras, F-16s with Saudi and American markings, and British Tornadoes sitting battle-ready on the tarmac. Pallets of supplies and materiel to be used for troops already on the ground were being fork-lifted from cavernous C-5s and stacked in endless, itemized rows.

Walking down the gangway of the Jumbo Jet at the MAC terminal at Dhahran International, we were marched in single file to a holding area where two huge tents with Arabic characters written all around the inside, were waiting for us to begin in processing. The dry desert heat, but surprisingly low humidity, took some getting used to at first. I dropped off my ruck and cracked open a bottle of water supplied for us by the Saudis, then listened to a briefing by a young G-5 Captain on acclimation of the new environment and aspects of the Saudi culture.

On one of our outside breaks, a Saudi bus driver approached Staff Sergeant Lisa Tanner, one of our tactical air traffic controllers, and I, asking for a light for his cigarette. Lisa passed her lit cigarette to him with her left hand, which according to Arab customs, is reserved for sanitary purposes. The right hand is used to shake hands and pass things to the other person. Lisa and I gave each other the *oops* look. It must not have been a problem to the driver, or he was making special allowances for the new Americans, for he thanked us both graciously, offering us each a piece of bread from the loaf he was carrying. It was delicious, a lot like French bread, tasting a little like pita.

All around us on the airfield were reminders of an impending battle. F-16s in flights of four screamed overhead, bunkers of concrete, sandbags and timber dotted the landscape, and a small army of soldiers in battle dress uniforms awaiting instructions and transportation to their next stop in this strange, new land.

An abandoned concrete plant on the outskirts of Dhahran would be our new home for the next two weeks. As the line of buses pulled through the perimeter gate, the old factory resembled a refugee camp. Scores of general purpose medium tents were erected in rows in the middle of the compound. Wooden four-place outhouses, constructed by an Engineer Battalion, were strategically placed at the ends of the rows of tents. The spartan accommodations looked a little primitive, but home is what you make it. A precursor to moving into the tents was to spend the first day and night in a rat-infested dirt-floor warehouse along with hundreds of other tired, sweaty GIs.

We all anticipated the same thing: the 24th Aviation Brigade's turn to rotate out to our assigned area of operations in the desolate desert countryside. It was part of the waiting game. Waiting for the ships carrying our trucks and generators to arrive at the port, waiting for the units arriving ahead of us to rotate into the tents from the warehouse, and of course, adapting to the strange new environment. During the heat of the day, between 1100 and 1300 hours, it was strongly suggested to relax, take a nap, or write letters home. A required siesta during a duty day was something to be treasured and taken advantage of, because when the time came, relaxation would be a distant improbability.

The units living in the crowded warehouse were broken down into categories. The folks in the middle were the happy ones; they'd been there for a while and knew how to adapt. Tiny personal cubicles were nicely arranged, with freshly laundered clothes drying on makeshift lines. Then, there were those on the periphery of the warehouse. They were the unhappy ones. The last ones to arrive. The blazing sun, and noise of the crowded compound hit full force at any given time of the day. The unhappy group had no choice but to resign to the heat, noise, and frustrations.

We joked a lot, making do with the absence of the creature comfort we'd grown so accustomed to. One of the favorite jokes was trying to figure out a way to collect uncomfortable duty pay, but we doubted Congress would approve.

Finally moved into our assigned tents, 2nd Platoon settled into another stage of homeless existence. Quite nice, actually. Each occupant of the tent fashioned a personalized corner of their little world, complete with pictures of loved ones. A technique for cooling drinking water to below room temperature learned from the brief stay in the warehouse, was to slide a one-liter bottle of water into a cotton sock, poor water over the sock, and hang it up in the open tent flap. The breeze cooled the water off much like a geothermal air conditioner. Nobody really complained too much about the primitive conditions, but rather adapted and overcame.

Marie's interpretation of events leading up to my deployment:

6 August, 0200. Another phone call in the middle of the night. Gary answered the phone, and I muttered something about I thought we'd left Germany where such phone calls were commonplace, and were little more than a bimonthly disturbance. I rolled over and went back to sleep.

0800. Gary pulled into the drive, and a bell went off in the back of my mind, which I immediately sent to that area of the brain reserved for denial. Never in twenty years had he ever left on alert and returned before regular quitting time.

As he came in the door, I tried to read his face, but what I saw also went into that space reserved for denial. I could tell when he kissed me that something was terribly wrong, but I refused to accept it. He said that he had one hour to pack his gear and report back to the unit; he was on his way to Saudi Arabia.

I said, "You're kidding, right?" He just looked at me and somehow I knew this was not one of his weird jokes. He was dead serious.

As I sat numbly on the bed, watching him pack his field gear and a duffle bag, I thought back to the beginning of our life together. Over the years, after the war in Vietnam ended, it always seemed that the idea of war would never appear again in our lifetime. Now I found myself with just six months to retirement, having to accept the fact that we would not be spared the agony of separation, due to hostilities in some far-off place.

I spent the entire day in denial. I figured this was just some bad dream that would go away by the six o'clock news. It didn't. He didn't return until nearly midnight that first night, and had to be back on duty by 0400. This schedule continued for several days. He wasn't getting much more than two hours of sleep a day, and I worried constantly about his health. He didn't take time to eat, and I knew he wasn't sleeping. Gary's in great shape; always making his runs and usually outrunning guys half his age. But the fact remains he's almost forty years old and the body will eventually rebel when abused.

By the second night of the alert, we decided we'd better contact our daughter Allison, visiting friends in Augusta. He'd been told he would be gone by the weekend, and it was important that he talk with her. It was decided she'd return and spend the last few days with her dad before he deployed.

Allison came home, but left again the following Sunday to be with her friends. Another week passed, and he was still here. Every day, the goodbye was said in the morning as if it were the final one. Allison returned home again, surprised to see her dad was still at home. Weren't we all?

The second week, I returned to denial. I hoped that any day, an agreement would be reached between our country and Iraq, and he would never have to go. Of course, we were all still being told that this was only an alert, but only a real idiot would have believed that. In twenty years of alerts, he never had to get shots or be measured for new uniforms. Who were they trying to kid, anyway?

Sometime during the third week, DCUs (desert camouflage uniforms) were issued and now were the new duty uniform. It was official. Those in DCUs were the ones going, and those in the old BDUs were staying behind. Not a lot of BDUs were seen around Hunter from then on.

During the weeks that the alert was on, I kept a pretty tight lid on my emotions while Gary or the girls were around. I knew it was up to me to set an example for the girls. After all, we all know that a PCS move is accepted only as well as the wife accepts it, so why should this be any different? I had times that I would well up, and the girls would always ask, "Are you okay, Mom?" I 'd shake my head yes, but inside I was screaming, "Hell no, I'm not okay!" Somehow, we made it through these terrible weeks.

Before the alert was over, I was in a place where I wished he'd just go. Saying goodbye for the last time every time he left the house was taking a toll. I don't remember how many times in the last couple of days before he left, I thought I'd seen him for the last time, only for him to come home late at night. Finally, I took him to work the morning he was to go to lock-in. When we got there, Top said it was off for a little while longer.

That evening, I drove my neighbor in to post so she could pick her husband's truck up at the gym. I looked everywhere for Gary, but nobody had seen him. I drove by the office, and everyone was there. I took him home long enough to take a shower and wash his DCUs for one last time. Later that night, he was locked in behind the fence.

Early the following morning, I was at the fence. I didn't see him anywhere, but I saw friends from other units who told me Gary's unit had not arrived yet. I left and went home very bewildered. Shortly after I got home, I got a call saying he was behind the fence. Master Sergeant Burk, the operations NCO for 1/58 promised to tell him I was on my way, and we would meet at a prearranged area behind the fence.

There I sat all day, in the heat and humidity, looking at him trying to memorize every detail of that weary face. We talked, and were joined by other couples from the unit. We all joked and talked of other, better times. Somehow, it still wasn't real that this was happening. How could this happen to us? I tried hard to understand that this was something he had to do. Not because he was ordered to go, but something deep down inside of him told him he had to.

I accepted that he had to go, because for the last twenty years, he's carried the guilt from never being ordered to serve in Vietnam. I personally viewed that as having lucked out, and still on occasion, have thanked God for that. He never felt that way about it, but it's always been hard for him to accept the fact he never went. Well, here's your chance, Babe, and even though I don't understand this need of yours, I accept it and love you for it.

I had just fallen into bed when the phone rang at midnight. It was Gary. He said they'd be flying at 0400. I started our call chain, set the alarm for 0230, and went back to sleep. At 0300, the girls and I were on the bleachers watching the troops file into a waiting plane. I couldn't make out anyone; they all looked alike. It was a pretty emotional time as the plane taxied toward the runway to the sound of "Proud to be an American". Tears rolled freely for the first time and I felt as if my heart had been torn from my chest. It was the most painful experience I'd ever had to deal with in my life thus far.

Since he's been gone, I've tried to keep a stiff upper lip. Somehow keep life normal for the kids. Each day gets a little tougher. I don't think it will ever get easy or tolerable, but I do my best. Of course, in the last twenty years, life goes very smoothly when Gary's at home. But, let him leave, no matter if it's just for overnight, everything goes wrong. This deployment has been no exception. To start with, I agreed to take in the CO's cat. I went in and got her at noon on a Friday. She took an instant dislike to our cat and Great Dane. That afternoon, when I left for work, she was hiding in a closet. By 1700, she was AWOL, and I didn't think we would ever see her again. I had no idea what I was going to tell Gary. That's not exactly the news you want to tell someone when they're so far away. I was really upset and mad at God about everything, and told Him so.

I had totally given up on the cat returning to our house and had decided I would have to go to the CO's neighborhood in a day or two and knock on doors to alert her neighbors to be on the lookout for the runaway cat. We have friends that live on the same street, and all the strays end up at their door because they feed them, so I thought I'd give them a call. Late the next night, thirty hours after the cat first went missing, she showed up at my door. She never went toward the door again, so she must have decided that the outside world wasn't any better than sharing the house with another cat and a five month old Great Dane that loved to chase them both around the house.

In the meanwhile, Sarah, our youngest daughter, who had never given us any real problems in recent history, decided now would be a good time to assert her independence. If told to do something, she wouldn't, and if told not to do something, she would. Guess she'll just have to learn that I still have thirty years of stubbornness on her and she won't win. I imagine she's starting to see that, since she's becoming more cooperative.

Now, Allison is a whole different story. She's very close to her father since he was her primary caregiver the first year of her life as I finished nurse's training. He'd get her up and ready in the morning, take her to the babysitter, and pick her up in the afternoon. She's never tolerated even the shortest separation, so I was expecting real trouble from that corner. Instead, she was very cooperative and didn't argue back with me or her sister. I thought she was handling the separation extremely well. I lived under this illusion for more than a week. I don't know if I ever learned just how badly she was doing inside, if I hadn't been punishing her sister for *her* behavior.

Once again, I'm at work, and I find out that Sarah had not done something she had been told to. I told her she was to write six pages out of the encyclopedia on Saudi Arabia as punishment. Of course, she proceeded to tell me how unfair I was , how I didn't love her, and she would do or say anything if I knew Allison had shoplifted at Eckerd's. I almost fainted away right there, but somehow managed to keep focused on telling her what I expected from her, and that it was to be completed and on the table when I got home from work.

I then asked to speak to Allison, and when she came on the line, I told her she had one chance, and one chance only, to tell me where she had gotten the necklace and earrings. She told me straight up what she'd done, and I then instructed her to get out her bible, and copy *Thou shalt not steal* a thousand times. It was to be on the table when I got home.

The next morning, I informed Allison she would have to write to her dad and tell him what she had done. I asked her if she had the money to pay for what she'd stolen, and if she had it, I would drive her to the store where she would have to tell the manager what she'd done and offer to pay for it. I also told her that if he wished to press charges, she would have to live with it. If she didn't have the money, I would call the police myself. Allison had the money, and the manager gave her a very stern talking to, and accepted payment for the stolen merchandise with the warning that next time, he would press charges. As we were leaving the store, I told her if there were a next time, she wouldn't have to worry about a store calling the police; I would personally call them. I don't think she'll ever do that again, at least I hope not. She knows by now that if I've never told her I'd do something, then failed to carry through.

I always knew I couldn't leave the girls alone while I worked. I only worked ten days a month, but a lot can happen in just that little time. It had been placed on my mind some days earlier to ask a young wife, pregnant with her first child, to move in with us. I had ignored this message of the heart, where I received all my messages from God, but now I knew I had to make some big changes in our lives. Gary wasn't coming home in just a few days. I don't know when he'll be home, and I don't know when we'll be told to expect the unit back. This is limbo, a terrible place to try to live.

Sharon has been with us for a week, now, and her husband Phillip, is deployed with Gary's unit. It's nice to have someone to share the day with, whether it's a good or bad day. We're all looking forward to the baby's birth, which could be any day now. I hope that somehow we can make it easier for her, I know she will miss having Phillip here to share the birth. I just wish we can fill some of the emptiness for her. Anyway, we're in this together, and that's easier than being in it alone.

There have been other frustrations and minor disasters here. The dog tore up the carpet in the front entryway. The house was only finished back in June, so that was classified as a disaster. However, it's amazing what a good carpet layer can do as far as repairing carpet. I have to look closely to see where it was restretched and spliced. The dog no longer stays in the house when we're gone, but now there's a big hole in the yard. I don't really care, because there's a lot of dirt around, so I'll have it filled before Gary gets home. All in all, we're managing to live one day at a time and deal with whatever comes up.

The worst part of the separation by far, is the feeling of helplessness to make life easier for the one you love. It breaks my heart to know the conditions he's living under. I send everything I can think of to make it better over there. It doesn't much satisfy the need to take care of him, though. That's been my number one job for twenty years, and I feel as if I've been laid off. I don't trust Uncle to take care of him. After all, I know him better than anyone else on this earth, and I hate having to turn him over to anyone else. The only one I'm willing to turn him over to is God, and I did that shortly after he left. So now, hard as it is, I'll wait and trust God to take care of him and send him back to me safe and sound.

Just back from Dhahran, let me tell you a little about how those battalion pukes live. They've contracted two compounds, one for the battalion, and one for the 18th Aviation Brigade, to whom we owe thanks for the airborne patch and the stately maroon beret. Both of these compounds are like apartment complexes of sorts. They were built for American and foreign civilian workers and their families. Each unit is air conditioned to the max, one has a pool and a party area. Each building is separated into several large bedrooms and spaced around a central courtyard. The main complaints I keep hearing from these people is the AC is too cold and the shuttle from the compound to their office is very unreliable.

The headquarters building was another source of comic relief for me. It was also air conditioned. Heaven forbid, our battalion should have to go to war, planning strategy while maintaining communications from a tactical position. These fools were wallowing in home-like luxury, maintaining the standard complaints they always had, and always will, about living and working conditions. Some have even gone so far as to comment on the lack of rental cars. It was priceless and laughable.

While trying hard to maintain the attitude of a professional soldier, looking on in awe at the amenities they were enjoying, I couldn't help thinking, let those poor bastards come with me to the outback and live under our conditions for one week. It would be a very humbling experience for them, to say the least.

Take heart, lads and lasses, for your TDY trip and palace life may be short-lived. I wondered how many of those folks realized that Major General McCaffrey, the 24th Division Commander and his Deputy Commander, Brigadier General Scott, lived in tents on a rock pile in the middle of the real desert, not too far from here.

I took particular comfort in the thought that my time in Dhahran was always only limited to specific missions, such as calling home from a satellite phone bank, attending staff meetings in the name of the commander, and awaiting transportation back to the 24th Brigade area about four hours north. I always felt strangely out of my comfort zone in the battalion compound. But, always taking the opportunity to invite the battalion staffers to come out and enjoy a real taste of field living at it's absolute extreme gave me a deep sense of satisfaction.

I ventured to think that for the most part, they couldn't wait to get back to where they felt they belonged, changing their attitudes about conditions in the outback: why radios go bad, why tempers flair, and why requisitioned mission-essential parts really needed a justification.

Having been deployed with the 24th Aviation Brigade, whom the 2nd Platoon had supported with Air traffic Control services back at Hunter, as well as at our tactical outpost about nineteen kilometers from Tahj, we were considerably protected from the ruthless politics of our battalion in Dhahran. As a matter of record, Colonel Tom Tackleberry, the 24th Brigade commander made it so the 2nd Platoon's new designation would be Charlie Company at some point during the alert.

Since we performed all the daily functions a company would: submitting a daily morning report, performing our own training, and requisitioning parts and services, the colonel said, "Hell, let's make 'em a company!" And so, the birth of Charlie Company, 1/58 AVN Regiment was hailed. However, this change brought on a lasting feud between 1ˢᵗ BN 58ᵗʰ AVN Regiment at Ft Bragg and COL Tack.

At a weekly staff meeting one September morning in Dhahran, I asked our battalion commander, Lieutenant Colonel Robert Mason, a field grade officer and former pilot who probably had little tactical experience, and assuredly limited knowledge of ATC procedures, for items I had never dreamed of asking for in the past. An upgraded tower like the new 7-Alpha would be a reliable exchange for the antiquated 70-Alpha, which had well-served dog units since the Korean war. For a long-term fix, the high-tech 7-A would afford greater radio capabilities, controller efficiency, and just a better situation all around.

Expecting raucous laughter from the battalion staff, LTC Mason's answer to my bold request was a direction to the C&E officer to research stock numbers and look into it. For a fleeting moment, I felt a surge of power in the palm of my hand I hadn't felt in a long time. The more I thought about it, though, the friction between LTC Mason and COL Tack may have been the catalyst for the decision to upgrade the old tower. I tended to think the latter held more juice than my well-planned request.

After the staff meeting was adjourned, the colonel wanted all commanders to stay for a G-2 (intelligence) briefing on the Iraqi build-up situation. What I learned from the beginning of the briefing, because they told me to leave, that it was classified, and any divulgence of its content would most likely compromise security, but I will say, Iraqi units were massing along the Saudi border.

Chances of anything of significance happening in this area very soon are very slim. The main purpose of the stare-down between Iraq and the coalition forces is to wait and see what impact the embargo had on Iraq, and to test the mettle and endurance of Saddam's forces, the patience of the multinational force and that of the Bush Administration.

Patience on the part of every American in the midst of the crisis in the Persian Gulf, could be categorized into two main groups. First of all, and most importantly, is the patience of wives, husbands, and families left behind in the states. Many, if not all, wanted the bullshit to end, their wives or husbands to come back home. Still, many felt that the US Military had no business there. However, that may not have been for anyone to judge fairly. We all wanted this to end quickly, or see it peacefully resolved. But the impatience of no productive settlement to date was in the forefront. Rhetoric abounded. Patience grew thin in the America public, not knowing why we were there, whether it was a political move or a military presence to stop the aggression.

People wanted results. To me, the answer was simple: we were doing what we've done throughout history. We were there to stop Saddam from trying to occupy Kuwait, to walk up and slap the bully, sending him packing, and tell him the United States and the world community would not tolerate those actions.

The other category consisted of the soldiers out in the desert, not necessarily the strategists or the planners of this mega-operation, but the real grunts, the worker bees. They held impatience about the vagueness of any long-range plans to just dig in and prepare for the unknown, inventory equipment in preparation to be spelled by another unit, or pack up bag and baggage and redeploy every nut and bolt. A complete reversal of the trip over, which could take up to ninety days. No one knew.

The capacity to endure hardships in the desert had been tested to the limits. In some cases, my own. Tensions from my job as Platoon Sergeant and Tactical Tower Chief, however minimal or controllable, caused me to slip into momentary depressions. Combine that with bad communications from home, and there arise situations only dealt with in one way--make a rather expensive phone call to get an instant response to a domestic issue interpreted by a bad letter from home. The mail turn-around was anywhere from two to four weeks from home to the field sites. I'd get a letter from Marie saying how badly she felt about being all alone, and her world is closing in on her. But that type of letter would be post marked three weeks ago. The sole thing on my mind was to get to a phone and talk to her. Phones were four hours away. The opportunity to make the trip didn't present itself very often.

When things come to a head before that call is made, those you work with and those who work for you inevitably become victims of that depression. Everything said and done is taken as a personal insult.

A black cloud that will not go away no matter how hard you try to make it disappear, forms over your sun. Everything is perceived as being wrong, and whatever you touch turns to crap. The desert closes in, and after a while in that gray funk, anything can bring you to tears. A gesture, a word, even a controllable situation. The world rushes in on all sides, and you just want to get out, get away. Nothing makes me glad I'm even alive. I took every precaution to keep that part of me very private.

Yes, a phone call can change everything; it can make the clouds go away and the sun come back out. When I heard Marie's voice on the other end of the line, and how I heard how things had gotten a lot better for her at home since she sent the distressful letter, my permanent smile returned. It could not be knocked off my face.

2 November 1990. Choking white borax dust clouded the troop compartment as the deuce-and-a-half churned its way through the desert. A quick-fix road had been graded by a heavy equipment engineer battalion months ago, but with all the heavy traffic the makeshift road had seen, potholes and sand pits in the road bed seemed to reach out and torture each passing vehicle.

Driving through this vast wasteland, the dirt road was used as a shortcut to the Damman to Riyadh Expressway, I was exposed to more outback than I had seen yet. I wondered how anyone could claim this parched no-man's land as sacred ground. Giant sand dunes, huge, ageless armies marching to all horizons at an unseen pace. Scrub bushes and fields of timeless volcanic rock occasionally emerge from the endless ocean of sand.

Nestled between the rolling dunes and rock formations were a myriad of tactical sites. From a distance, these field installations appeared as rocks or large clumps of brush. At closer scrutiny, communications antennas could be seen towering above the mound-like cammo nets concealing trucks, vans, or tents, like desert flowers sprouting from rock piles.

Tank trails paralleled the rocky, dusty road on both sides. Occasionally, a column of tanks would pass by in the opposite direction, choking us with a blinding momentary sandstorm. Another column of M-1 Abrams, commo APCs and Bradleys raced up alongside the truck with relative ease on the sandy trail, but the ancient deuce-and-a-half was no match for the powerful machines. Racing over the rough landscape like power boats racing the waves, the column glided past, then veered off into the open desert, reminiscent of one of Rommel's battle formations. The line of heavy battle machines disappeared into their own dust cloud toward the western horizon.

Impressive, to say the least, from an outsider's point of view, the existence of these machines in the desert lends an air of impending confrontation with an unseen enemy. To the casual observer, it gave a feeling of relief to know they were around to do the job they were designed to do and more.

Those guys deserved the praise of us all. They had one of the hardest jobs out here in the desert. Their days were filled with training missions under the blazing sun, eating dust and sand with every turn of the road wheels of their iron steeds. Sleeping in cramped crew compartments, atop their vehicles, or in the man-made shade on the ground alongside the tracks, catching a few winks in shifts while being ever vigilant for snakes and scorpions, and monitoring the crackling Fox-Mike radio for instructions to move out to the next grid coordinate. A valued part of the overall battle picture, a tanker's life, in a tactical sense, was one of the harshest out here. Here's to the nomadic world of the tanker.

18 November 1990. It's been nearly ninety days since I kissed Marie and the girls goodbye. An eternity, of sorts. Some days, time passed by quickly. Other days, at a snail's pace. Each one rougher than the day before. The hardest thing about being out here is having no defined reason for it. Couple that with word from Brigade of an indefinite deployment, and problems arise.

A lot of people out here have constructed barricades of all types. Oh, physical barricades springing up daily were an ever-present indication of the inevitable. Sandbag-bunkered trenches, tent fortifications, even changes in the countryside gave a quiet warning of increasing readiness.

What became gradually harder to deal with were the emotional barricades people were constantly building. Constantly fortifying. Guys who were friends back at Hunter, and even when we first stepped foot on this foreign soil, guarded their conversations, psychoanalyzing every decision made by NCOs or officers, and being unconcerned with long or short-range effects of any type of human interaction. Long story short, some folks just stop giving a crap about anything. Tempers flared at the slightest provocation, tears flowed openly and privately. I can certainly attest to the latter.

Several weeks ago, an indiscretion was committed by two members of Charlie Company which had a domino effect on several others. No more coed tents. Evidently, some folks weren't mature enough to accept things as they were and to deal with each other as soldiers first and a burning desire to satisfy physical needs second. Out of fifty-two soldiers in Charlie Company, seven marriages ended in divorce by the end of our deployment.

From the outset of this deployment, I naively tried convincing myself that the coed tent arrangement was not an important issue. The male-female camaraderie was an accepted thing, and that such moments of weakness between male and female would never come to pass in Charlie Company. I guess I was wrong.

Along with the gravity of this situation, however miniscule compared to the impending bloody war, the mere aspect of a small group of non-battle hardened soldiers thinking, working, and living in such close proximity on a daily basis, caused everyone in this tiny colony to react to every action, play favorites, make irrational decisions effecting others, and ever fortifying that emotional barricade folks had built around themselves.

Along with folks' behavior patterns, the countryside had changed a bit. Each dusty trip down the road to Dhahran revealed changes in unit presence nestled in the hillsides. More and more encampments were springing up where before, nothing stood but empty desert wasteland, dried up wadis, and wind-carved rock formations standing in silent sentinel over thousands of years. Air Defense units with Vulcan systems, artillery units with Howitzer batteries and MRLS systems, all stood in quiet readiness pointed toward the north. Eerie feelings enveloped those who witnessed these advanced tools of war being readied. At this juncture, it was only a defensive measure. But who will fire the first shot? Who will pay the price? Will it be worth it? These questions and more burned indelibly in a soldier's mind in the desert. Moreover, how will it affect my family and me?

The past two days have been filled with events far from the mundane. Just a kilometer to the south of us were two medical battalions and a graves registration unit. Several C-130s and Blackhawks, along with hundreds of medical personnel have been involved with a mass casualty exercise. Our packed sand and gravel runway had evolved from helicopters only to a Hunter Army Airfield type environment. But, Hunter boasted of a two mile long runway, and nearly a hundred acres of taxiways, parking ramps and hangars. The big boys couldn't land here, but with C-130s landing and departing with such frequency, each creating a dusty hurricane, new dimensions were added to the preparations for war: resupply, stepped-up training, and increased air traffic.

As a matter of fact, the outdated but still functional Korean War era aircraft landing control central our guys were using had finally been replaced by a freshly-rebuilt, still in the crate air traffic control tower, our somewhat promised 7-Alpha. This state of the art gadgetry was only ten to fifteen years old. Aside from any technological advances made here in the desert, life was pretty much day to day.

I also thought a lot about my family back in Savannah. The mail system, the way it was, has, if anything, damaged the communication Marie and I have had for the past twenty years. If I received a letter dated 14 October from her on 30 October, what she said in the letter may not apply on the 30th. Same goes for me. I may really be in the pits when I write her, but when she gets that letter, I may have regretted some of the things I said. My one regret as far as my family was concerned was that my being deployed to a potential battle zone, I felt that I'd abandoned them; forsaken the ones I love.

The guilt I felt was a mixture of sadness and regret for them, for me, and for us as a family. The 'us' at this time, although hindered by a sloppy mail system, but existed strongly in our hearts. The guilt of leaving everything up to Marie; each decision about our lives, finances, raising the kids, and taking care of our new house, rested squarely and heavily on Marie's shoulders. The emotional pain was unbearable at times, yielding to private tears.

Marie was convinced through some recent pictures I'd sent depicting my spartan life in the desert, that I wasn't the same man she kissed goodbye at the fence at Hunter. The gaunt, unrested, and sallow-eyed stranger in those pictures couldn't be me. I've aged since I left her, she'd say. I didn't look well, she'd comment. To an extent, it was true. I celebrated my fortieth birthday in this arid wasteland with my surrogate family. I worried a lot about the people and equipment I was responsible for. You can't sleep restfully on a non-flexing army cot. However, I've slept much better on the air mattress Marie sent me a couple of weeks ago. Eating food intended for short term sustenance does not help people gain weight. Primitive eating conditions, a common outhouse to relieve yourself, desert heat, and the constant threat of war, all combined to make me appear far past my years.

The following passage is entitled "A Child's Fear" written by Sarah, eleven years old:

My worst nightmare became a reality last September. The person whom I have lived with for the past eleven years was gone. I don't mean dead or anything like that, I just mean that my dad was sent to defend oil in Saudi Arabia. I was very depressed for a few months, and I wouldn't do anything my mom told me to. I would just do the opposite of what she told me to do.

Then we had a young pregnant woman named Sharon move in with us to help us a little. But she never did anything but yell at our Great Dane puppy, Duchess. She lived with us for almost two months, then Mom asked her to leave because after the baby was born, she never helped us at all. Of course, I was having to look at a complete stranger sleep in my room, that and she didn't ever let anyone in there. I was kind of glad when she was asked to move out.

I had a very tough Thanksgiving weekend, because Mom had to work, so our friends the McNarys had asked us to spend Thanksgiving with them. Christmas was even harder to get past. The Christmas Cantata that our church choir performed every year was hard to sing without Dad there. My sister, Allison and I stopped playing our instruments, and we rarely went to church anymore.

It is January now, and two days ago the deadline for Saddam Hussein to get out of Kuwait came and went. It is the 17th now, and the air war began yesterday. I was so glad to hear we were the ones that bombed first. We had went to two special prayer services Monday and yesterday. I cried a lot at both meetings, but our friend, Theresa Brown comforted us. Allison and I did not go to school on the 17th because Allison had a very bad cold, and I stayed because I had not slept the night before.

I am watching the news, and I am growing very scared at the moment, I had begun to cry. I have gone to my room and flung myself onto my bed and cried. I cried myself to sleep, and in the morning, I awoke in my clothes. It is the 23rd now, a week after the war started. My mother had said it seemed like a year. The operation in Saudi Arabia is now called Operation Desert Storm. Don't think I will see my dad before my birthday which is April 23rd. I do think I will see him before my mother's birthday, which is June 3rd.

My school has support groups for children whose father is in Saudi Arabia. We had another meeting today and we watched the news for half an hour. I don't think that the group does anything to help us, but they sure do try hard to comfort us.

I have this tooth problem, you see. The dentists say that it is very minor, but it sounds like a major operation. It starts out as a very dull pain, then it spreads throughout my face, jaw, and head. Later on it becomes very painful, because my jaw and head hurts like crazy. I really hate it when it happens at night, because I don't get any sleep. I don't complain to my mother because she said there is nothing we can do about it until I stop growing. I will have to have my bottom jaw shortened and my top jaw spreaded a little.

This letter of pre-planning was thankfully never needed.

Dear Marie,

There is nothing I can say to you and the girls I haven't already said, I love you all very much and look forward to seeing us all together again. In the event I don't return from Saudi Arabia, which is highly unlikely, in addition to the provisions of my last will and testament, I leave you, Marie, my loving wife and mother of my children, two choices for my burial. My first choice would be dependant upon your decision to remain in Savannah. In such case, I wish to be interned in the Bonaventure Gardens Cemetery in Savannah with full military honors. My second choice is Arlington National Cemetery. Oh, please make sure I have a nice view of the Potomac.

This request may or may not be viewed as a legal and binding document. But Marie, I've known you for twenty three years, and have never know you to back down from anything. When and if I return from the Middle East, I will owe you, Marie, so much that I could never repay you, except with my deep love and commitment to a life-long companionship. See you real soon.

Love, Gary

Marie's letter to friends after the deployment, calling for care package items:

Dear Family and Friends,

Please forgive me for not writing very much right now, but I just wanted to let you know that Gary has left for Saudi Arabia. These are difficult times for those that are going and those that are left behind. I ask that you pray for us and our country, and if you get a few minutes, please write to him at the following address:

SFC Gary J. Smith
481-60-2574
2/A Co. 1/58 AVN RGT
APO NY 09675

Also, please note that the name of our street has changed to Albert Street. Anyone interested in sending a care package, I have included a list of items that will be most needed. However, packages will not be able to be sent over for about a month since the priority will be to get the men and equipment there first. Letters can be sent right away, but can't weigh more than twelve ounces and contain no pornographic materials, tobacco, or religious materials. Mail will be censored going either way.

Following is a list of items that would be appreciated and/or needed by Gary and his troops:

1. Pre-sweetened Kool-Aid packs
2. Powdered Gator Ade to help prevent dehydration
3. Disposable razors
4. Toothpaste/toothbrush
5. Fly swatter
6. #50 sun block
7. Blistex lip balm, Vaseline to coat exposed skin
8. Paperback books (remove cover if a female is on it)
9. Travel board games, or other small games
10. Postage stamps, envelopes, paper, pens
11. Bar soap, shampoo, deodorant

What seems to be most important to those leaving is the knowledge that the people of our country support them and what they are being asked to do for each of us in this country. Gary has requested that our flag be flown be flown until our troops return and that blue and yellow ribbons be displayed. The blue represents our troops and the yellow, the hostages. The flag can be flown twenty four hours a day if lit at night, to make a political statement. Since this meant so much to him, I'm sure he would appreciate it if each of you do the same.

Love,
Marie & Girls

The infamous *last letter* which I had taped inside the lid to my footlocker:

My Dearest Marie,

This letter is meant for you to read only in the event of my death. Hopefully, all my personal affects should accompany it.

As I write this letter, I have tears in my eyes, thinking of you, Allison, and Sarah. If you are reading this, I know your worst nightmare has come true, but saying goodbye from the Great Beyond will be no day at the beach, no pun intended. Please be strong and help our kids to grow. Our love for each other has seen a lot of good times, and some bad. I want you to remember only the good times.

Let's go back in time and think about how we grew together. The physical love we shared in the beginning grew slowly into a strong, ever progressive relationship we could both be happy with. With that, we shared a sense of satisfaction that not many marriages could claim.

New Jersey was a strange new world for both of us. All we had was each other, and we grew stronger because of it. San Antonio was a very romantic time for us. Our marriage was maturing, and so were we. Panama was interesting, wasn't it?

Maryland was a bit of a setback. I was weak, but you were strong for both of us. When I wanted to move to Ft Rucker to become an Air Traffic Controller, you supported me, but you didn't much care for it. For that, I apologize for putting our lives in a voluntary tailspin. We weathered that one too, though, didn't we?

We both made friends at Ft Rucker just as we did everywhere else we've been. Our live continued to change and improve. We bought our first house and had real roots for a while.

Germany and our trips across Europe, was another romantic time for us, just as San Antonio was. Bad times set in again. This time, money was a major issue, and separations began to rear there ugly heads as wedges between us. But, with those short separations, our love once again grew stronger.

Savannah, by far, has been the sweet spot in my life, how about yours? We've waited a long time, and the right moment for our dream home together. Now, my days are filled with those sweet memories.

That last night at the fence continues to be a bittersweet memory. The guilt I felt about leaving was ten, no, a thousand times greater than the feelings of betrayal as I backed out of your folks' driveway and headed for San Antonio, watching you set on the back steps with your heart in your hands and tears streaming down your face.

Babe, I want you to promise me one thing: please continue with your life as soon as possible. The wounds inflicted by this terrible war will heal with time, but I know memories of years past will dominate your life. Please don't let this happen. Be there for the girls. Teach them independence. When you're ready, fill your days, and nights, with more sweet memories. You owe it to yourself, but please don't fall in love with someone who won't allow you to be Marie, or hurt you in any way. I will not tolerate this, and if it's possible to protect you from the Beyond, I will.

Honey, if you're reading this, please know that I didn't die a coward. Being here, either in Saudi or Iraq, wherever I ended up, was the greatest sacrifice either one of us could make. If my life was taken, it was to save the life of one of my soldiers. I could never sacrifice another's life to save my own, but understand I'm no hero, either. I remember what you said, look out for yourself, but I could never do that and live the rest of my life wondering what I could have done differently.

I can say no more . I've written my feelings down and feel certain you'll agree with them for the most part. Goodbye, my love. Please continue to live your life. My faith in God and my love for you has only grown stronger here. I no longer fear death. I'll be smart, but if my time comes, I will not be afraid.

I'll always love you,
Gary

A small contingent from Brigade departed TAA Ginger to drive ahead into Iraq. At 0500 hours on 25 February, six vehicles had left the old assembly area aided only by the faint red spots of the blackout lights of the vehicle ahead. Some drivers were issued PVS-5s, the newer, more reliable night vision goggles.

The SP time on Tapline Road, known to the Geodetic Survey folks as the Trans-Arabian pipeline, was 0600 hours. The seven mile trip took the better part of an hour in the darkness. The moon was totally obscured by a high cloud layer, making the going painstakingly slow.

At 0555 hours, the small convoy pulled onto Tapline Road, halting to regroup at the SP. The vehicle ahead of us, a CUCV Chevy Blazer, was losing his lights. An electrical short in the wiring system had caused an excessive drain on his batteries. I suspected one or both alternators were on their way to alternator heaven. As luck dictated sometimes, I was instructed to load my ruck in that vehicle and return to TAA Ginger with the driver, a young Spec 4 by the name of O'Neal, a battalion cook. As O'Neal and I crossed the pipeline and headed back down the trail towards Ginger, the engine quit. Sand and dust played havoc with fuel and air systems out here, and proper maintenance was not always able to be performed the way it was back at Hunter. With no juice to recrank the tired Blazer, the damn thing became a casualty of six months in the desert. The roads, the sand, and all combined elements had taken their toll on HQ1.

O'Neal and I, after checking everything out, determined that mixing a twenty-four volt Saudi battery with a military issue battery wreaked havoc on the charging system. It could work in an emergency, but over time, the damaging difference in amperage was phenomenal.

It began to rain on the lonely desert road. At first, an annoying sprinkle, then a steady shower. The day wasn't ending well, nothing had gone as planned, and things started closing in on us. After about forty-five minutes, two vehicles came churning down the trail. As they closed on us, we saw that the lead vehicle was a Deuce from 1/24 hauling a four hundred gallon M112 Water Buffalo with a Blazer in trail. They stopped to help us get the disabled Blazer running again, but they had no slave cables. Enroute to the Division supply area at Log Base Charlie, they offered to call back to Brigade when they reached their destination, and notify our units of the situation. Right, I thought, wondering why this damn thing wasn't checked out any better before the Brigade marched up north.

A few minutes later, a couple guys from 3/24 Maintenance stopped to help. They also had no cables, but they fixed us up with two brand new batteries, putting us back on the road. Finally arriving at the Tactical Assembly Area Ginger, we both notified our units of the breakdown on the road, and lined up in the convoy with the unreliable Blazer. Not a good advertisement for Chevrolet.

In the lineup, there was little to do but check tires, oil, and rearrange and check our equipment in the cargo area, check food and water, then try and catch a few winks. The time was now 0900 hours, and the new SP time to head out was set for 1400.

The time to roll out for the trek north had finally arrived. It was 1435 hours. Radios, engines, tires, and loads had been checked and rechecked. Engines were idling, and occasional revving of the deuces' engines sent plumes of acrid black smoke into the still afternoon air. A great day for a long drive north.

Making its way back to the pipeline, the mile-and-a-half long convoy snaked its way onto the highway and eased along Tapline Road. The anticipated right turn to the north was still twenty clicks ahead.

The convoy slowly turned right off Tapline Road onto a hard-surfaced desert trail leading into Iraq, that was constructed by a combat engineer unit. The flat, smooth road almost resembling a six lane highway, and could have been used as a runway, led the convoy past hastily constructed POW camps and MP checkpoints.

The Iraqi border loomed ahead like a wall of solid rock in the flat desert. A sign had been placed along the left side of the road, sort of a trademark of the engineer battalion that carved it out of the desert. The sign read, "Welcome to Iraq, Shortcut to the Euphrates, Combat Trail X-ray, Courtesy of the 16th Engineer Battalion." These guys had quite a sense of humor.

From that point on, everyone was more on guard than they'd ever been. This was real. We were in Iraq. The 24th Aviation Brigade would help provide the cork for the bottleneck in the valley between the Tigris and Euphrates Rivers, the only escape route for retreating Iraqi forces leaving Kuwait.

We had crossed into Iraq around 1705 hours that afternoon, 25 February. It began to rain again, first a light sprinkle, then a steady downpour. The road had turned from a flat, smooth hard surface to quagmires crossing partially dried up wadis. These lake beds were being churned to peanut butter by hundreds of trucks and vehicles ahead of us, leaving a danger zone for those to follow.

Darkness fell like a cloak over the desert, revealing only a few obstacles on the road: rocks and mud holes. The weakened electrical system of the CUCV I was driving worsened with every mile. The blackout lights worked intermittently, until I hit a bump in the road. It seemed like I needed to hit another bump from time to time to get them to work again.

The road had slightly improved from what it was before. A maintenance stop was signaled, so, pulling off to the side of the road, O'Neal and I set up a defensive position. The original driver of the lightless vehicle, O'Neal shared a little of his shade tree mechanical expertise, and got under the hood with a flashlight, checking wiring, batteries and fuses, trying in vain to determine the cause of the problem. From then on, night vision goggles would have to be worn.

As the convoy headed north again, the new batteries in the Blazer were totally drained. No lights, no wipers. Only an occasional flicker of the idiot lights on the instrument panel. A seemingly simple problem, but when wearing NOGs, a flickering idiot light was like a strobe in the eyes, shutting the goggles down.

2045 hours. It was still raining steadily, and the wind was picking up. The convoy had halted on the dark, muddy road to allow a tank column to cross somewhere up ahead in the darkness. I just realized I was supposed to take another PB tab at 2030. Fifteen minutes late wouldn't be that big a deal. If I could remember to take those pills on time, it would be a lot easier, but forgetting to take them on schedule meant having to readjust the dose times. Hell, I forgot what they said those little pills were for. As I recall, they were to stave off any effects of a chemical attack. General McCaffrey had put the whole division in the heavy, charcoal-lined MOPP gear weeks ago as a precaution against such attacks.

0035 hours, 26 February. After what seemed like endless hours of mud bogging in the darkness of night, through pouring rain with a truck with no lights or windshield wipers, and the NOG frames cutting into my temples, we came across a huge open area. Vehicle lights in an unfamiliar pattern glowed like beacons through the blinding rain.

By the time I realized some of the trucks up ahead had tried to negotiate the open area, which was in reality a muddy lake bed, another partially dried up wadi, they were hopelessly bogged down in a random pattern. I fell into the same trap, mired to the axles. In trying to free the Blazer from the unforgiving mud, the engine quit. The batteries were completely gone, and the CUCV was dead in the water, causing our worst fears to become reality. The mud was knee-deep in places; the persistent rain turning the bog into oatmeal, lying in wait for any brave soul thinking he could navigate through it with no problem.

Our truck was about number seven on the list for assistance from a five-ton wrecker assigned to rescue the disabled vehicles. The rest of the convoy slogged ahead, trying to meet their objective by very strict wartime convoy checkpoint procedures. That was the scary part . Here, O'Neal and I were, deep inside Iraq at night, during a storm, the damn truck was stuck tight and wouldn't start, not so much as a solenoid click. We joked about singing a couple refrains of *"Kumbaya"*, just to get through it all.

Our turn finally came for assistance from the wrecker. He jumped us off and hauled us out of the muck. He directed us to meet up with the freed vehicles at a point about a quarter of a mile up ahead on the right side of the lakebed.

A great sigh of relief came when I realized one of the trucks was Charlie Company's supply pickup driven by Ernie Murray, a muscular, boisterous Spec 4 from Baltimore, Maryland. The other truck was the environmental control van for the new 7-Alpha, driven by one of the young controllers, Mac MacCullough.

The area we met up in was occupied by heavy, tracked vehicles of the 197th Infantry Brigade out of Stewart. Among those vehicles, an M88 tank retriever sat idling, an M113 APC being towed by the 88, and thank God, an M-1 Abrams. The heavily armored mother hen was watching over her brood, her turbine engine a beautiful sound above the howling of the wind and clatter of the rain against the windows and top of the Blazer.

Through the night, the storm increased in intensity. With the Abrams idling close by providing security for exhausted, mud-covered soldiers, we crawled into cabs and backseats of our rescued vehicles for a couple hours of welcome, yet fitful sleep. Remembering we were deep inside Iraq, any rest would be minimal, yet adequate. Everyone remained on their guard while taking turns sleeping.

Dawn was only a few short hours away, and the Shamal storm showed no signs of letting up. A far better chance at regrouping, repairing damage to the ancient trucks caused during the hasty night march north, and safely reaching our objective, could all be achieved after a couple hours sleep during daylight.

The main body continued the night convoy to their first objective, leaving behind stuck or disabled vehicles and their crews to provide personnel and equipment security.

Thoughts of being stranded during a storm in the dead of night, in a potentially hostile environment, were far outweighed by both the camaraderie of the people left behind, and the ever-present ideal that we were all that much closer to going home. When things started going badly, the new catch phrase was, "Saddam, don't start with me!"

What everyone deployed to Desert Shield, then later, Desert Storm had been through the past six months, particularly since the air war began, and now the ground war, affected each of us in such a way that hardship and decision making took on whole new meanings.

0345 hours, 26 February. I'm exhausted now. I surrender my entire being to the loving arms of slumber. Dawn will bring the beginning of a whole new adventure. Thirty-six hours have passed since the last jump was initiated. Not much sleep was allowed in that time. It couldn't be, there's a war on.

0630 hours, 26 February. We hit the road with our small convoy, after being slaved off the wrecker again. That was really getting old. Down the road about five clicks, we linked up with 1/24 and a medical battalion convoy. Again, we fueled up the trucks and checked loads.

Got some damn good news about a plea to Iraqi troops by Radio Bagdad to pull out of Kuwait to the north and assume positions that were taken up on 1 August. Come on ahead, boys! At least three divisions of angry American and Coalition street fighters will be waiting for you. Our objective was their only way out. However, that elation was overshadowed by the tragic news of a SCUD missile landing on a Pennsylvania National Guard barracks in Dhahran. Forty soldiers were unaccounted for.

The 1/24 convoy with our small group in trail, departed the refueling and maintenance area along MSR (main supply route) X-ray, affectionately known as "*The Combat Trail to Hell*", at 0910 hours. The rain clouds slowly gave way to blue skies, but the wind was still blasting out of the east at an estimated fifty to sixty miles an hour. A steady north-eastern progression of the convey was lain siege by the howling winds and blinding sand of the first Shamal of the season, or the first one we'd experienced. Shamal, literally translated from Iraqi Arabic, meant *'Devil Wind'*. Couldn't have been a more apt description. The wind drove the sand with such force that even on the inside of the closed CUCV, the gritty feeling and taste of sand in your eyes, nose, and mouth became an increasing aggravation. At times, it was hard to breath.

Forced off the road by zero visibility, the convoy again halted, hoping to wait out the brunt of the storm. Problem was, sometimes those storms were capable of raging for days, transforming the sun into a dirty brown glow. To get lost in a storm like that could spell disaster to the impatient, unwise, or ill-equipped. Word was passed down over the radio to assume tactical positions, hunker down and rest for a few hours.

1730 hours. We finally pulled into our first objective, FAA (forward assembly area) Donna. Exhausted and dusty, nonetheless we were happy to see the rest of Charlie Company. The vehicles were parked in a wide circle, facing out from the center. We relaxed, set up guard posts, then briefed Top and Cpt Kelly about our little road trip.

It was a bright, moonlit night. A little chilly, but livable. The howling winds had died down considerably. Thanking O'Neal for the company on our unforgettable trip, I fixed a spot on the tailgate of Ernie's supply Blazer to grab a little sleep. O'Neal and I joked about our experiences on the road, then bid each other a good night.

0200 hours, 27 February. Guard duty from two to three. Sergeant Fay Ross was on the list before me, so I let her know where I was at so I could relieve her. The tailgate wasn't all that comfortable, but I knew it would only be for one night. I curled up and tried to close my eyes.

Ross. Now there was a real piece of work. Aside from always hitting on the warrant officers in battalion, she was just plain lazy, caring more about her own comfort than her job. She was one of the controllers in the 7-Alpha, who would throw a hissy whenever I'd give her a job to do.

She had always resented that I kept sending her to the Learning Center at Rucker for low test scores.

0600 hours. The 24th Brigade convoy departed Donna for FAA Tammie, about forty clicks down the road to the northeast. One thing that truly amazed me about traveling in the desert with maps that really show no prominent objects, but yet an exact point can be found within a hundred meters. Just about every command vehicle in the Brigade had in their possession an amazing little piece of technology called a Global Positioning System, or GPS for short. This device worked off a satellite feed that determines a preprogrammed grid and pinpoints locations, sort of like a reverse homing device. One drawback is it won't work at certain times of the early evening when the satellite wasn't in a useful window.

0930 hours. The convoy arrived at FAA Tammie, and after circling the trucks, we began setting up the control tower. About halfway into the installation, Top came over to inform us we had two hours to SP (start point) to the next objective. God, I thought, please let it be Dhahran. At that point, we were advised of the reason. The 24th would be part of the *door slammers* in the Euphrates River Valley. At 1425 hours, we continued northeast on MSR Yankee toward our next objective.

After driving through all kinds of terrain including quicksand and swamps on both sides of the road, and another damn mud bog, we finally came out on a six lane expressway heading northeast towards the Euphrates.

Periodically, we halted on the highway to allow other convoys to pass. Never before had I witnessed such a massive exodus of military hardware. It was a very strange feeling to be part of such a momentum.

We reached our next objective at around 2130 hours. A plateau two clicks east of the freeway would serve as our assembly area for the night. Wagons circled, guards posted, I was checking the bushes for a good place to relieve myself, when I noticed something strangely familiar, yet foreboding, lying on the ground in the moonlight. A closer look confirmed it was an RPG, a Soviet-made rocket-propelled grenade launcher. I'd taken photos of that weapon while I was stationed at Aberdeen Proving Grounds. Further inspection of the area led to the discovery of yet another abandoned Iraqi weapon, an AKM assault rifle lying in the sand.

Afraid to touch either weapon, thinking they may have been booby trapped, I hollered at First Sergeant Larry McJunkin, who was using a bush to relieve himself a few meters away. We both thought it best to let S-2 know about the discovery, and let them handle it. The RPG was full of sand, and luckily, there was no rocket loaded in it. However, the rifle was loaded with a thirty round clip. Its charging handle was packed with sand, but could have been easily cleaned out, restoring it to its lethal state.

As the sun cast a golden glow on the landscape, the boys from S-2 allowed us to take trophy pictures of Top and I holding the abandoned weapons. I entertained thoughts of rendering each weapon inert, carrying them back to Hunter to use as training devices, but S-2 flatly denied our request, stating they would turn them in to Division for disposition.

Word spread quickly that ATC stumbled on some Iraqi weapons, and guys began scouring the area looking for more remnants of the Iraqi retreat. Items of clothing, helmets, parkas, canteens and pistol belts, and even shoes and boots were discovered.

0730, 28 February. We slowly made our way back to the freeway, but remained on an access road running parallel to it until we found a good opening to enter the six-lane. Several clicks down the road, we entered the freeway, encountering the first Iraqi vehicles destroyed in the Allied air attacks. Orders from Central Command during the air war, were to kill anything that moved. In the next several kilometers, what we witnessed was not far from the truth.

Crossing a cloverleaf exchange, a cluster of burned-out vehicles were partially blocking our path. The six-lane was littered with burned hulks of cars, trucks, buses, and motorbikes. Clothing and shards of metal had been blown in all directions by the violent explosions. The A-10s and Apaches had done their jobs well. The devastation and carnage, the aftermath of the air attacks, were etched in everyone's memories. Burned out hulks of vehicles, bodies of dead Iraqi soldiers, some lying grotesquely alongside their charred trucks, all gave silent witness to their hopelessly feeble attempt in escaping the death from above.

We'd driven a few kilometers northeast on the freeway, when the convoy commander was given word by higher headquarters to do an about face and head south to an even newer objective. Exiting the highway onto a secondary road revealed yet more gruesome remains of air attacks. Charred hulks of troop trucks and an armored personnel carrier littered the exit ramp. As we entered the secondary road, a small group of Iraqi soldiers were walking alongside the road, some barefoot, all wearing mismatched and tattered uniforms, and one carrying a white flag on a stick in surrender.

Earlier, we'd received a blanket radio call to disregard the surrendering soldiers and keep moving. They were carrying bottles of water and packets of MREs as we passed, waving and blowing kisses at us. It seemed as if they were thankful to Allah that this frightening war was over for them, grateful to the Coalition for releasing the terrible burden overshadowing their lives. It was reported by BBC that *'Murder Battalions'* followed frontline troops, enforcing loyalties to Saddam Hussein, forcing these exhausted and terrified soldiers to continue fighting. Any Iraqi soldier caught trying to surrender or defect to coalition forces would be immediately and summarily executed. At that point, over fifty thousand POWs had been taken, and forty of the forty-four divisions had been destroyed.

0600, 1 March. Sergeant Jim Jackson, a controller, mechanic, former helicopter pilot, and all around go-to guy, woke me up hollering, "It's over!" The cease fire was announced and all offensive action by the Coalition Forces was basically suspended. There were a lot of happy faces at the assembly area that morning. Folks milled around swapping war stories and thoughts of going home. BBC reported silence on all fronts.

About three clicks down the road, a cluster of still burning trucks blocked our path, causing the convoy to detour off the road to the right. Just as we came upon the burning remains of a Mercedes five ton, Top wanted to stop and take a picture of it. He had just snapped the picture when I noticed a wooden box of RPG rockets on the ground between the burning truck and our Blazer, also in flames. A fraction of a second later, one of the rockets launched itself across the bow of the Blazer, impacting about fifty yards to our right, scaring the Bejesus out of us all.

Further down the road, were still more burning remains of trucks and cars, and bodies of dead Iraqis strewn about. Off the road to the left, were a pair of shoeless feet lying on the ground, a grotesque reminder of the horrors and cruelty of war. Packs of wild dogs picked at human remains strewn along the opposite side of the highway.

The entire morning was a sobering experience for everyone. The stark realism and human tragedy of war was stunningly brought to light for us all, and for some, the very first time. Some will never be able to release from their memories what they saw and experienced that day. If Larry had not wanted to stop and take a picture of that burning truck, I'm certain even today that the four of us in that Blazer would not have survived.

15. New Horizons

My decision to retire from the US Army came relatively easily. Countless letters and phone calls to Marie during the seven months in Saudi Arabia and Iraq during the Gulf war outlined my plans to retire once it was over. A simple rationale for me was, *I'm just gettin' too old for this stuff.*

I passed the twenty year mark in the Army, celebrated my fortieth birthday, and rejoiced, through the mail at being married for twenty years during the seven month deployment. Because I was the oldest soldier of fifty-two men and women in Charlie Company, I secretly enjoyed being called "Dad" by my peers and subordinates. Those jokers even presented me with a big pan of brownies generously frosted with a gallon of chocolate pudding, all liberated from the cooks at the 1/24 Battalion mess tent. Of course, they tried to convince me the barter system was used in the procurement, but I had my doubts with theses guys. Garnished with M&Ms from home, the top of the chocolate surprise read, *"Happy 40th, Dad"*

Redeployment for the 24th Aviation Brigade came on 17 March, 1991. Our job in Southwest Asia was done. The brigade convoyed south to Dhahran, stopping along the way to rendezvous with our tactical Air Traffic Control team. SSG Lisa Tanner, the team chief, and SGT Jon Fallon had been near Basra, lending ATC support to a medevac unit throughout the Ground War. Exhausted, but ready to fire away with tales of war, they were herded to CPT Kelly's tent for a mission debrief.

Khobar Towers in Dhahran was our final marshalling point before driving the vehicles to the port for shipment back home. A luxury apartment complex located near the National Oil Company headquarters in Dhahran, the Towers became the target of terrorists truck bombers, tragically ending the lives of nineteen US Servicemen and one Saudi national on 25 June 1996.

Three long, arduous days were spent cleaning the desert grit from trucks, tents, camouflage nets, and ATC equipment, before inventorying everything and packing it for shipment back home. Phone calls were made to let loved ones at home we would be on our way soon.

Well, the party was over. The long, weary, but jubilant line of troops began boarding the white Tower Air 747 for the long flight home. Unlike troops returning from Vietnam alone, not as part of a unit, the proud 24th Aviation Brigade commanded by COL Tackleberry deployed and redeployed as a huge family.

Following a brief stopover at Rhein Main Air Force Base in Frankfurt to fix a faulty cargo door and enjoy a beer and bratwurst gratefully provided by the USO, we continued our journey across the Atlantic. I called Marie to inform her of our latest estimated time of arrival. She responded with a mixture of elation and acceptance of the harsh reality of how plans can change quickly, "The Brigade wives have already given us three or four dates and times you'll be getting in. When they call back to tell me you're inbound to Hunter, I'll be there to meet you. The girls are excited you're coming home. I love you, can't wait to see you again."

Frankfurt was behind us now. Most of my three hundred-some comrades in arms were fairly quiet for the remainder of the flight to Hunter. A perfect opportunity for sleep and overdue relaxation was taken advantage of, on the heels of seven months of twenty-four-seven *go, go, go.*

I drifted in and out of fitful sleep, my mind racing with thoughts of running up to Marie and the kids, scooping them up in my arms, telling them how much I love and missed them. Home…going home.

The constant whine of the 747's engines slacked off, I felt the airspeed and altitude drop as we entered the airspace around Savannah. Almost home. COL Tack's booming, familiar voice came over the intercom, offering a few last words of fatherly advice about coming home to families, friends, and loved ones.

"Go easy, ladies and gentlemen. It's been a long time. Don't try too hard to be a parent or spouse. There'll be some changes, and adjustments will have to be made. Love them. Be patient with them, as I know they will be with you. Oh, one more thing. I would like everyone to stand fast when we pull up to the DAGC point, so that all our Vietnam vets can deplane first. We owe them that."

Tears began welling up in my eyes, as my thoughts and prayers went out to these guys. Of the thousands of men and women who served in 'Nam, some never quite made it back. The Gulf War lasted all of a hundred days through the air and ground battles, and the men and women who served, received a hero's welcome complete with parades, flag-waving and hugs from total strangers. Returning Vietnam vets were forced to be spirited through airports in civilian clothes amid taunts of, "baby killers!" It was time to make this right.

Looking around the cramped cabin through tear-filled eyes, discovering I was not alone, I couldn't see a dry eye in the crowd. A reverent silence fell over the wide-bodied cabin as the Vietnam vets of the Brigade stood and marched slowly with heads held high to the gangway door. Applause for these men began with one proud observer, then another, and another, until the entire plane rocked with cheers and applause.

Spotting Marie and the girls milling around the back of the crowd inside the huge DAGC hangar, I jumped and waved at them. Pushing my way through the throng of soldiers being greeted by their loved ones, I ran into the open arms of my family. We engaged in a long-awaited group hug, just standing there, not uttering a word. Sarah, our youngest, finally said, "Can we go home now?" We all laughed at her candor as we headed for the car.

For months following, my thoughts remained on retiring from the Army, making plans for the future, and watching us grow back as a family. The more I talked about retiring, Marie would keep asking the obvious, "What's your plan? You've got to have a plan."

Plan? I guess I need to have a plan. Over the years, I'd completed several college courses, eventually earning an Associate Degree in General Studies from Harford Community College, in Bel Air, Maryland, while stationed at APG. I was enrolled at Armstrong State College in Savannah, to pick up a few more core courses. The plan was set; attend college full time using my VA benefits, and choose a career field on the way. Radiological Technology sounded like a good secure field, so I registered for Rad Tech school, with classes beginning the end of September.

The big retirement date, 1 September 1992, came and went, and I slowly melded into life as a civilian. I missed the regimentation of the Army, to a degree, but I found several new friends at Armstrong who were either active duty, retired, or a military spouse. We all found that common ground, a bond so peculiar to life in or around the military.

After a year of being a Rad Tech student, I wanted something different, so I applied for and was accepted into the Elementary Education program. That was a better choice. I saw myself with a much brighter future as a teacher than as a Rad Tech.

During my tenure as a student teacher at White Bluff Elementary, I interviewed for a teaching position at Largo-Tibet Elementary. I was hired, and began teaching second grade in August of '96. At the beginning of my second year at Largo-Tibet, I was shifted to another school in the Chatham County system, Georgetown Elementary. Enrollment numbers were way down in the first two weeks of school, so, like in the Army, I was placed where I was needed the most.

The spring of my third year at Georgetown brought about more changes. I was greeted one early May afternoon in 2000, with a job offer Marie had received from a Gastroenterologist she had worked with in Savannah. He would be opening a satellite clinic in Vidalia, and wanted Marie to be his office manager. A growing community of about twelve thousand, the Sweet Onion Capital was less than a hundred miles northwest of Savannah.

The challenge of selling the house, moving to a new place, meeting new friends and beginning a new life was nothing new to this Army family.

"Why not?" I said. "After all, I moved you all over the world for twenty-two years. Now, it's your turn."

Our house on Albert Street in Savannah was on the market for four days, when it was shown and the buyer made an offer. We accepted the bid, and shockingly, it was for the listed price. After several trips to Vidalia, we found the house we would enjoy for years to come.

I located a fifth grade teaching position at Lyons Elementary in Toombs County, but after the first year, my contract for the 2001-'02 school year wasn't renewed.

Frustrated, confused, and angry at the *good ole boy* system so prevalent in these rural Georgia counties, I confronted the principal, Barbara Flowers, asking why my contract wasn't being renewed. I couldn't figure it out; my evaluations were all satisfactory. What wasn't right about this?

Her only response was, "I don't have to tell you, but if you'd like, you can request an answer in writing to the county board office." "Whoa!" I thought to myself. "I really don't even want to go there. A person has to learn when and where he isn't wanted."

So, after polishing up my resume, I sat out to the surrounding counties: Wheeler, Montgomery, Treutlen, and Tattnall, in search of another job. It was the middle of February, 2001. I tactfully made it clear to the administration at Lyons Elementary that I would need at least two days a week to locate a new teaching position. I made up my mind this would be no easy task. Two full days a week were dedicated to schools in each county, visiting their respective Board of Education offices and elementary schools.

Towns in each of the four counties I traveled to were steeped in rural Southern tradition and charm. Streets of many of the small towns in the four-county area were lined with live-oak trees, bordered by manicured lawns adorned with dogwoods and azaleas. The houses fit a broad range of construction from antebellum mansions, fifties style craftsman's, to the standard brick ranch.

Far from the stereotypical redneck ogres depicted in movies and on TV, I discovered when I stopped to ask directions in those small towns, the people were really quite nice. It helped, though, to assimilate a southern drawl. Some folks may have found that down-home speak sort of flattering. Having been stationed south of the Mason-Dixon Line the better part of my military career, it came rather naturally.

Vowing not to give up hope of finding a new teaching post sooner or later, I carried my resume and ambition into one county board office and elementary school after another. I was given several interviews, each sounding very promising. Each interview, however, left me with an empty feeling and the token, "Thanks for stopping by. We'll be in touch if anything opens up."

Towards the end of May, I received a call from Gena Wilson, the Assistant Principal of Reidsville Middle School, on the behest of Lisa Turner, the principal, to come in for an interview. A position was available at the Tattnall County Alternative School, teaching at-risk kids. A great opportunity, I envisioned. I learned a little about alternative schools during my years as an undergraduate student.

A successful interview with Mrs. Wilson and Mrs. Turner led to a contract signing for the upcoming school year, teaching ninth through twelfth grades, with a possibility of teaching the lower middle school grades later on. My teaching certification was for kindergarten through the fifth grade, and I was a little apprehensive about having the ability to teach high school aged at-risk kids. My concern was first validated, but then alleviated, during my first few years at the Alternative School.

My first day on the job working with the high school students was far from boring or any normality. Passing out different colored folders to my new charges, I innocently presented a red folder to a young Mexican student, the son of a migrant farm worker. The young man of sixteen, went ballistic, throwing chairs and cursing. I thought, "Man, what did I get myself into?" It took the middle grades teacher, two paraprofessionals, and myself to get him to calm down. No amount of intervention helped, so we ended up calling the police to have him removed from the classroom.

When the dust settled from the outburst, I was quietly informed by the veteran teacher that the color red represented an opposing gang color to this child, triggering his violent behavior.

As time progressed, I became more educated and aware of street slang and mannerisms used by these kids. The vast majority of my students came from strife-ridden single-parent homes, or were products of the Department of Family and Child Services system. The key to successfully dealing with these kids on a daily basis was patience and understanding. Many of them came to school because their probation officer told them if they didn't, they'd end up in Juvie, or that school was the only place they could eat a meal. The other side of the coin indicated that some kids sought shelter at school. Shelter from an abusive home. Shelter from the only life they knew, one of hardship, crime, and violence.

The school board elected to close the alternative school at the end of May, 2008. Due in part to state budget cuts, because the number of students enrolled at the alternative school was at an all-time low. It would not be feasible to keep it open any longer. Fortunately, over the years, Mrs. Turner encouraged me to earn an interrelated Special Education certificate in order to properly service the learning-disabled students being sent to the alternative school. This inadvertently laid the groundwork for what was to follow.

Marie and I were eating at Shoney's in Vidalia one evening in early June, when we ran into Mrs. Turner and her husband Jackie, a Vietnam veteran who served proudly as a Marine in Vietnam. I always like running into Lisa off duty. She always had a smile and a bit of good news. Tonight was extra special.

"I know the alternative school is closing, and I know you've been on a serious job hunt. I have a Special Ed slot open at Glennville Middle. If you're interested, it's yours," she offered. Lisa had come out of retirement to assume the principalship at Glennville middle.

Not believing what I was hearing, without even thinking twice, I said, "I'd be delighted and honored. Just remember," I added, "that you're the one that pushed me to get that certification." I was ecstatic. Go out to eat, and get a job offer. Life is good!

16. The Final Mission: A Dedication to All Vietnam Veterans

This passage is dedicated to an old friend, Barney "Pete" Philpot, a fellow veteran, who has carried the horrors of the Vietnam War for too many years. Here's to you, Barney, and all who served.

The chopper droned through the early morning mist cloaking the coastline south of the demilitarized zone. The eastern horizon of the South China Sea was painted in a gray haze, creating a continuous flow from sea to sky. The pristine beauty of the fog-enshrouded Au Shau Valley to the west looked deceivingly calm. The 1ˢᵗ CAV UH-1 Huey wove a nap-of-the-earth course south from Quang Tri to Da Nang, using the cover of green jungle valleys, then occasionally climbing to fifteen-hundred feet above ground level to seek less dense, cooler air.

It was April, 1968. The Tet Offensive, a disastrous turning point in the war in which the will of the American forces had been intensely tested, had taken place in January. Pete's year in 'Nam was up, and he was on his way to climb aboard the Northwest Orient *freedom bird* parked on the tarmac at Da Nang Air Base. One final throw, however, was that the pilot of the Huey wanted him to do the job he had done for the last twelve in this jungle hell, one last time. He was to defend the chopper on its flight to Da Nang.

Pete was an Army Security Agency communications specialist, also serving as a door gunner with the 1ˢᵗ Cavalry Division (Air-Mobile) operating out of a base camp at Phu Bi Hue, near Quang Tri. Each mission he flew left an indelible mark etched in the book of American lives saved by suppressing enemy activity on the ground. With his M-60 machine gun blazing away with a fusillade of fire, Pete yelled over the roar of the chopper's gas turbine engine the positions of his beleaguered comrades on the ground, as the pilot banked sharply for running landings into one hot LZ after another. Even with the gunship still sliding to a turbulent halt in the grassy savanna and following the purple marker smoke, trapped American soldiers awaiting evacuation would come barreling from the cover of a tree line, tossing rucks and wounded buddies onto the floor of the chopper.

Back at the base camp, everything that happened on the day's mission was emotionally weighed. To the soldiers fighting the battles, and to the pilots flying choppers in and out of danger zones, the missions were not measured in success, but in the cost of human lives and the number of bullet holes in the aircraft. In brief respites between these missions, weapons were cleaned and checked, letters to loved ones at home were written. The nightmare of war was momentarily forgotten with a cold beer while strains of Dylan, Hendrix, Steppenwolf, The Who, CCR, and an endless stream of artists whose music of the times aided in the escape of daily tragedy in this jungle hell, courtesy of AFVN Radio.

Somehow, amidst the chaos surrounding each mission, Pete managed to sort through his feelings about the war in Vietnam. Political motivation was not the reason he and thousands of young men just like him were fighting and dying in this far-off land. These people had been fighting for their freedom from foreign invaders for nearly two thousand years. To think a world power could step in and solve these age-old woes quickly and easily was pretty unrealistic. Wanting to see world peace and being a part of the endless fight for democracy was a better reason. The cost would be great, however, both in tax payer dollars and human lives.

Pete recalled a portion of President Johnson's state-of-the-union address on television back in '65. He was only eighteen at the time, but he could remember well when LBJ announced that he had doubled the forces on the ground in Vietnam, and would not hesitate to send more if they were needed. He added that as American men and women went to far-off lands to fight and die for that foreign country's freedom, we all had learned at a terrible and brutal cost that defeat does not bring safety, nor does weakness bring peace. Peace, Pete concluded, had to be the single most important reason he was there.

The only people with anything to gain politically were the upper echelons of leadership, and the lawmakers back home. Their reasons were simple. Building a military career on successful missions, or a political career with a good foreign policy base, was critical. Additionally, profiteers supplying the *beans and bullets,* the needed supplies to continue fighting the war, realized a two-sided benefit. They got rich and gained political influence at the same time.

Time seemed to stand still on that morning flight to Da Nang. The steady whine of the Huey's transmission and turbine engine shut out all memories of the war. Gazing past the cocked and ready M-60 resting on its bipod mount in the open door of the chopper, to the jungle carpet passing beneath the aircraft, Pete was transported to another place and time.

Growing up in Hogansville, Georgia, a small mill town fifty miles southwest of Atlanta and the home of a U.S. Tire and Rubber plant, Pete experienced life in this middle class blue collar community to the fullest. He played fullback for the Hogansville High School Green Waves, helping his team to win the 1963 state football championship. An all-around athlete, Pete was a catcher on the high school baseball team, and a star runner on the track team. A handsome and muscular young man, with sandy brown hair and a winning smile, he was voted "most talented" during his senior year. Standing a slight five-foot-six, but with a quick temper and lightning reflexes, Pete was emulated by his friends, yet a power to be reckoned with on the field of play.

Pete's given name was Barney Lee Philpot, named after his father, a machine operator at the tire plant. Folks started calling him Pete to save confusion, so the nickname stuck. The Philpot's were respected in the community of God-fearing, yet politically indifferent blue collar workers. The war in Vietnam was a subject that most residents of Hogansville avoided. World War II, Korea, and ultimately Vietnam had claimed the lives of several native sons, and war was simply not a topic for discussion.

"Small arms fire at my four o'clock! Take 'em out , gunner!" The serenity of the flight and Pete's thoughts were suddenly shattered by the pilot's frantic shouting through the flight helmet intercom. Dazed and shaken by the sudden uproar, Pete jumped to his feet, shaking the cobwebs from his mind. Quickly checking the charging handle of the M-60, Pete scanned the area the pilot had pointed out. Everything had become automatic for him in the past year. There was no wasted motion. There was no time. He was the aircraft's only defense.

Spotting a muzzle flash in a small break in the dense jungle canopy below, Pete raked the area with a steady, sweeping spray of tracer rounds. Braced against the rapid recoil of the machine gun, with his jaw set and fire in his steel blue eyes, Pete continued his vicious attack like a man possessed on the unseen sniper below as the pilot put the Huey through a torturous right banking turn. The tracers sliced through the dense vegetation, chewing up small trees and bushes, kicking up great clouds of dust and white smoke, marking certain death for anyone in the vicinity.

The pilot continued a slow right turn as all eyes searched the jungle for any signs of movement. Finally, banking left to resume their southerly course to Da Nang, the pilot called over the intercom for a quick damage and nerve assessment.

"Well, whoever he was, he's deader'n a mackerel, or he ran down his rat hole. Good job, gun. Thanks!"

"Wish I could say it was all in a day's work," Pete replied in his boom mike. "Think we got him. All the same, I'll be glad as hell to get on that plane."

Pete slumped down into the webbed seat facing the side door, wiping the sweat from his face with a bandana tied around his neck. Feeling the chill of sweat trickling down his neck and back, he thought to himself as he pensively twisted the ends of his full mustache. *Yeah, I'll be glad as hell to get on that plane.*

The sun was much higher in the sky when the Huey touched down at Da Nang Air Base. Heat waves shimmered off the tarmac in the mid-morning sun, creating mirages of standing water. The humidity hung in the air like a wet blanket. With no shade on the flight line, it was worse than being in the bush.

The crew chief was the first to exit the aircraft. With fire extinguisher in hand, he moved his extended fingers across his throat, signaling the pilot that it was okay to shut down. Adding to the standard hand signals, his index and middle fingers pointing toward his eyes, he then gestured to the starboard side of the tail boom.

Curiosity getting the best of them, the pilot, copilot, and Pete bailed out to see what the crew chief was pointing at. What they saw sent chills up their spines. The sniper had stitched a line of AK-47 bullet holes the entire length of the tail boom, miraculously missing the drive shaft, tail rotor, forty-five degree gear box, and by the grace of God, the cabin.

A blue and white Northwest Orient 727 crouched like a great eagle watching over her brood in the shimmering heat on the tarmac. She offered sanctuary for the battle-weary and a reward for a job well done, a trip home. Pete shouldered his duffle bag, and looking across the hot asphalt flight line at his freedom bird, inhaled slowly and deeply. He glanced back at the helicopter crew standing shoulder to shoulder, watching their friend walk away. No one said a word, only exchanged glances in silence across the tarmac. They'd been through a lot together in the last year, and felt a close bond. They would always share that common bond, one of brotherhood.

"Good luck back in the world," the pilot offered, finally breaking the silence.

"Thanks. You guys ever make it to Hogansville, look me up," Pete returned.

A flight of F-4 Phantoms screamed overhead. Pete briefly glanced skyward, then turned and slowly walked toward the line of GIs snaking its way to the base of the gangway stairs leading to the open door of the jetliner. Behind him, he heard a young, eager-sounding voice call out to the crew of the chopper.

"Mornin'! Name's Henderson. I'm your new door gunner."

Hesitating momentarily, Pete chuckled to himself. *"Yeah, welcome to 'Nam, buddy."*

"Put your duffel bags on the white line!" bellowed the loadmaster, pointing to the single line of bags stacked like a giant cord of firewood.

"Get out a copy of your orders to give to the NCO at the top of the stairs!"

A chorus of groans arose from the line of tired soldiers waiting in the hot sun. The only thing they really cared about was getting on the plane and going home. They had fought and almost died in this strange country, and now some knot head wants to shout orders like they were a bunch of cherries right off the plane!

Handing a copy of his rotation orders to the sergeant standing in the plane's doorway, Pete wound his way down the crowded aisle looking for an empty seat. Finding one just aft of the wing, he sat down next to a young lieutenant wearing highly starched khakis. There was quite a mixture of uniforms on the plane that morning. Some guys had come right out of the bush wearing their jungle fatigues, giving the crowded cabin the aroma of a football locker room after a hard-fought game.

A little self-conscious about his own bedraggled appearance, Pete glanced through his flight sunglasses down at his own sweat-soaked fatigues with the sleeves rolled up to mid-forearm, then at the lieutenant's neatly pressed uniform. No comparison, he thought. The guy probably sat on his butt at MACV Headquarters, and got a damn combat patch for it!

The 727 roared down the runway, struggling to reach rotation speed in the heavy, tropical air. The very second the rumble of the wheels on the runway gave way to the cushion of rushing air beneath the wings and fuselage of the plane, a seemingly endless cheer rang out from one hundred and seventy grateful voices.

Wheels up and locked, the freedom bird turned on course for San Francisco and the real world. Behind them was the green hell, the nightmarish reality of war. Some would leave that all behind them in that far-off land, treating it as simply a year's departure from reality. For others, it meant a trip home in a body bag. Sadly, though, for Pete and thousands just like him, the war in Vietnam would continue. It would hang like a specter, torturing their souls for years to come.

The captain's announcement came over the cabin intercom, subduing the excited anticipation of landing at San Francisco in less than two hours. "We regret to inform you that due to some type of antiwar rally at San Francisco International, we've been instructed by the Military Airlift Command to divert to Seattle-Tacoma. Again, we apologize for any inconvenience."

This time, instead of groans and complaints about the incompetence of the system, uproarious laughter spread throughout the cabin.

"Hell no, we won't go!" yelled a young private sitting in the tail section. More laughter rose up in the crowded cabin.

"Now I know how I ended up in 'Nam!" bellowed another comedian. "I forgot to burn my damn draft card!" The spontaneous laughter fueled even more comments until it appeared everyone on the plane was after their turn in the spotlight, their fifteen seconds of fame.

The plane was descending on final approach into Sea-Tac. The relentless roar of the four jet engines was now a quiet whisper, and the feeling of weightlessness had set in. The flight from Da Nang was exhaustingly long. The mood of the returning warriors had ranged from anger at the military system, to laughter and joking, to the now somber, apprehensive air that hung over the cabin like a dark cloud. No one really knew what to expect.

It was around 8:30 in the evening, Pacific time, when the plane taxied to the MAC terminal. Storm clouds threatened overhead, an ominous sign of things to come for these battle-weary soldiers. There was no fanfare, no brass band, no families or loved ones rushing up to greet them. It was like landing in the middle of the night deep in enemy territory. Civilian clothes were issued to each of the soldiers on the plane from Da Nang that night, an attempt to disguise and blend them into a hostile society.

The war in Vietnam was far from over. For many of these brave men, it would go on for years back home. For the next twenty three years, Pete kept his suffering very private. He became accustomed to hiding the emotional pain spawned by the horrors of war he had seen and lived. He was unable, however, to block out what an enemy bullet, rocket, land nine or grenade could due to human flesh and spirit.

Memories of catastrophic events were but a small part of Pete's psychological turmoil. The other part was multi-facetted. Primarily, American troops looked at themselves as liberators of oppression. The problem with that was the Vietnamese people and their government had had their fill of oppressors and liberators for centuries. They simply tolerated the presence of the Americans and their allies. The Viet Cong lived and worked among the Vietnamese populace in order to weave their deceptive web of death and destruction, representing the eyes and ears of the North Vietnamese Army. No one ever knew who the real enemy was. He was a child wanting to play catch. He was an old lady carrying groceries. He was death itself.

Next, were the protests on the home front carried out by radicals nationwide, using the debacles of war to blast the government, destroy American patriotism, and treat all Vietnam veterans as outcasts, baby killers, and dregs of society.

The specter of war was buried deep in the recesses of Pete's memory since his return. Huge gaps existed in his recollection of certain times, places, and friendships. In August, 1990, that demon was reanimated, opening old wounds Pete and thousands of others had tried to heal for years. Some of these gaps were being filled in by the war in the Persian Gulf.

Another inconsistency for Pete was that he never knew how effective or lethal his work as a door gunner was. Accuracy and coverage were no problem. Trying to eliminate an unseen enemy offered no resolution. He never saw them fall. He wondered how many of these new high-tech warriors would experience that same empty feeling.

The curtain went up on Desert Storm in January, and the bitterness and animosity that Pete and countless other Vietnam vets had harbored for so many years resurfaced, becoming more lucid than ever. Pete feared that the foul stench of resentment and indifference toward these forgotten American heroes would continue to fester. To an extent, his fears were alleviated. With each passing day of troop deployment to the Middle East, the fervor of long-lost patriotism killed by the Vietnam war was being revived. American flags were being flown everywhere. Americans were proud to display their praise and support of our troops fighting and dying in Desert Storm, and the Bush Administration's tough stance on international terrorism.

Pete was elated when the soldiers who fought in Desert Storm went off to war and would return as whole units, unlike the soldiers who went off to fight the Viet Cong went over there and returned alone... and sometimes even died alone. The unfortunate ones relived the war back home for twenty-five years.

Pete wept openly at times, tears of joy for renewed patriotism in the hearts of Americans. He also wept bitter tears of sorrow for the young men and women who would be escorted home in flag-draped coffins, and for further public denial of what was so tragically earned and so desperately deserved for the countless sacrifices made in Vietnam. Recognition and appreciation for a job well done, and for so many, the supreme sacrifice, was all that was ever asked. But the war continued to rage. The embers that smoldered and burned fitfully for a quarter of a century burst into the full flame of remembrance. For the next four years, Pete continued to battle the revived apparitions of the war in Vietnam.

In mid-March, 1995, Pete was encouraged by friends and fellow veterans to travel with them to Washington, DC to visit the Vietnam War Memorial and lay to rest for good the ghosts created so long ago by that tragic war. After extensive soul-searching, Pete fearfully set out on a journey that would change his life.

DC hadn't changed all that much from what Pete remembered from trips made there while stationed at Fort Meade before shipping out to 'Nam in '67. Some new buildings and monuments dotted the landscape: the new Air and Space Museum, the Vietnam Memorial wall, and the Three Soldiers statue. The same age-old buildings and monuments he remembered still remained in sentinel over the nation's capitol. The crush of tourists hadn't changed, either.

There were noticeable differences, though. There were no antiwar rallies, no hippies dressed in bellbottom jeans, tie-dyed t-shirts, or draped in beads and flowers. In their place were Vietnam vets dressed in jungle fatigue shirts proudly displaying unit combat patches and medals earned in battle. Not wanting to portray the stereotypical image of a battle-dressed vet, Pete chose to dress conservatively, wearing a yellow sport shirt, gray slacks, and a brown leather bomber jacket.

On the edge of a small pine tree stand at the northeast corner of the reflecting pool stretching east from the Lincoln Memorial, the monument of the Three Soldiers stood silently watching guard over the ominous black granite wall, the Vietnam Memorial. The wall took the shape of a huge, gently sloping inverted "V", with a brick walkway in front, along its entire length. A grassy berm ran the entire length above and behind the granite wall, sloping gently to the ground at each end.

The mood at the wall was one of deep reverence. Visitors spoke in whispers, seeking familiar names etched in the polished black granite. Uniform-clad veterans tearfully reached out to touch a name on the wall, seeking closeness to a fallen, yet unforgotten comrade. Others paid loving tribute by placing photographs, flowers, or heartfelt handwritten letters on the ground next to the wall. If anyone wept openly on discovering a familiar name, or was simply caught up in the abounding emotion, it was not uncommon for a total stranger to walk up and embrace them, offering tender words of encouragement.

Pete stood silently before the gleaming black wall, scanning the names through a haze of tears. He was alone at that section of names, but he felt the gentle touch of a hand on his right shoulder. A sideways glimpse confirmed it was someone's hand, not just his imagination. Hesitantly, he glanced back at his own reflection in the polished granite. Standing to his left, and slightly behind him, was a figure his own height and build, clad in sweat-stained jungle fatigues with the sleeves rolled up to mid-forearm. He wore a green bush hat, aviation style sunglasses, and sported a full mustache. Hanging loosely around his neck was an olive drab bandana. Appearing much younger than Pete, the young man looked intriguingly familiar.

Purposefully, the young man spoke in a soft, familiar whisper. "Hard, isn't it, brother?" Pete stared into their reflections, nodding his approval. By now, tears flowed freely down Pete's cheek.

"You can't do this all by yourself, my friend," the young soldier offered, gently squeezing Pete's shoulder. "No one can. Well, gotta go now. Welcome home, buddy."

Wiping the tears from his eyes, Pete spun around to thank the soldier and introduce himself, but the young man was nowhere in sight. He quickly scanned each end of the monument only to find a half dozen Japanese tourists taking snapshots of each other, and a group of school children being ushered along by their teacher. The young soldier had vanished as quickly as he appeared. *Welcome home*", Pete thought to himself, echoing the words of the mysterious young stranger.

There was an eerie decisiveness about the encounter at the wall. Pete felt a certain finality, a closure to a very painful chapter of his life. Slowly making his way to the end of the brick walkway, he climbed the grassy knoll behind the granite wall. He stood there momentarily, with the wall at his back, holding his head high. Breathing in the fresh spring air, Pete felt the strange sensation that the memories that had tormented him since 1968 were behind him. His private war was over.

Epilogue

When I began writing this book in 1986, the idea came to me from all the drama I encountered throughout my assignment in Germany. Just about everyone I was associated with in Ansbach had at least one personal issue that effected the lives of others. Some folks, whether superiors, subordinates, or peers, at times displayed comedic responses to tense situations, while others, well, to quote Sergeant Kurt Messina, were *"back stabbin', belly draggin', tail bitin' varmints,"* who went out of their way to make the lives of those around them miserable. There was an astonishing degree of dissention among the members of 3rd Platoon,1/58 Aviation Regiment, that would plant the seed for me to document interesting interactions between them, and with me.

I recall relating to one of my co-workers one day, that, "I could write a book about this place." That comment was made in jest, but later on, I thought, why not? After purchasing a word processor at the PX, I claimed a quiet corner in our apartment, and went to work. The original story unfolded on the flight to Germany. However, as time passed, I lost interest in the pursuit of this literary endeavor, filing the uncompleted manuscript in the dusty archives of my home office. One of the reasons for putting it aside for many years, was the disenchanting thought that kept haunting me: Who the hell would be interested in reading my life story?

As my teaching career developed, I noticed that more and more symptoms of my afore-diagnosed Gulf War Syndrome, were beginning to effect my actions and judgement in the classroom, my relationship with my wife and daughters, and ultimately my decision to retire from the teaching profession. Searching for viable options to an undignified, and untimely departure from teaching, after much soul-searching, the choice was made to submit to my school administrators, a letter of intent to retire. Pulling no punches, and with all honesty to my supervisors, I cited the problems I'd been encountering for years. Retirement was a far better alternative than continuing down a bad road.

Dusting off the yet unnamed, unfinished manuscript, and finding my old diaries in the attic, I was determined to come up with a finished product, one that I could be proud of, something I could dedicate to brave men and women who have fought and died in foreign wars, particularly, the Vietnam war. *Patriot Son* gradually evolved into just that.

However dramatized for the sake of heightened interest by a fellow veteran who someday may pick up this book, and say, "Hey, I was there!", or, "I've done that!", all names depicted in this memoir have been changed. However, all events, circumstances, locations, and my personal reflections, all existed as reality. I began keeping a diary when I first arrived in Germany, and maintained it throughout the seven long months during Desert Shield and Desert Storm, writing down, sometimes in my own unreadable short hand, things that I experienced and people I was associated with, knowing I'd never forget either one. Yet, some of these situations and associations I'd just as soon purge from my memory.

The intent in sharing these memoirs is for the purpose of praising those who have served proudly in the US Military, those brave warriors who have fought or fallen in battle, and those who have battled the specter of war for so long. Welcome home, brothers. May God bless you and keep you.

Senior picture, Marshalltown High School. Summer 1967

Basic Training, Ft Lewis, Washington October, 1970

Photography student, Ft Monmouth, New Jersey, 1971

Sarah (in diapers) and Allison give Dad some physical therapy

Germany, 1988, following the death of my father
and my promotion to SFC

SGT. Jon Fallon and I in the 7-A during the Gulf War.

Rookie teacher. Second year, teaching 2nd grade

Retirement is good!